WILLIAM SHAKESPEARE:

The Life of King Henry the Fifth

"And gentlemen in England now a-bed
Shall think themselves accurs'd they were not here"

THE LIFE OF KING
Henry V
BY WILLIAM SHAKESPEARE

————————◦◦◦————————

The Arden Text, edited by Herbert Arthur Evans;

with a general introduction by Mr. Evans

and a special prefatory note by Mark Van Doren;

illustrated with paintings by Fritz Kredel

based upon the film version of the play created by

LAURENCE OLIVIER

————————◦◦◦————————

New York : The Heritage Press

THIS EDITION IS DEDICATED TO

Laurence Olivier

FOR WHOM, IT IS NOW OBVIOUS,

THE BARD OF AVON WROTE

THIS PICTURE-PLAY

Preface

Henry V is the one play of Shakespeare's which he might be said to have written for the movies. As a matter of fact he said so himself, or something like it, in the prologues he arranged to have read before his several acts. These famous poems—and nothing in all the play is better than the poetry they contain—are apologies for the limitations of his stage. His stage was not limited for drama, as no stage is when a real dramatist commands it; but it was limited for spectacle, and *Henry V* was in his view chiefly a spectacle. More than anything else he wanted his play to seem splendid—as splendid as England, as glittering as the young King who in the early years of the previous century had cut such a handsome swath through the meadows of chivalry. And Shakespeare was afraid that even the Globe Theatre, with all of its resources, would fail to provide the panorama thus envisaged.

In none of his other plays does he have the same concern. Accepting the limitations of his medium as any master does, he goes ahead to make those limitations the source of a triumphant success. *Hamlet* does not ask for a real Elsinore, *A Midsummer Night's Dream* for fairyland itself, or *King Lear* for better lightning than sound effects and tremendous verse may conspire to produce. *Antony and Cleopatra* occupies the whole of Egypt, but does so through feats of language and miracles of characterization. Only *Henry V* among the plays of Shakespeare is restless with desire to be set in another place than the Bankside spot where Falstaff had been so perfectly at home. The reason may be that Shakespeare was through with history as drama—*Henry V* comes last in a great series of chronicle tragedies he wrote with kings as heroes, to be succeeded almost at once by *Julius Caesar* and *Hamlet* wherein a different order of personal crisis is explored —and impatient with the bulky materials it had burdened him with. Or there may be a dozen other reasons. The fact, however, is clear. Shakespeare wants an unlimited scene. And since the verse of his prologues can only suggest such a thing, he dreams of a new medium that might make it possible. Doubtless his dreams never included our movies. But the waking man would have been most entertained by what Laurence Olivier has done with *Henry V*.

Why else should he have begun by asking for "a Muse of fire that would ascend the brightest heaven of invention"? Why should he have insisted upon

> A kingdom for a stage, princes to act,
> And monarchs to behold the swelling scene?

He can only regret his limitations of linen and wood.

> But pardon, gentles all,
> The flat unraised spirits that hath dar'd
> On this unworthy scafford to bring forth
> So great an object. Can this cockpit hold
> The vasty fields of France? Or may we cram
> Within this wooden O the very casques
> That did affright the very air at Agincourt?

He can only resolve to work as best he may with words upon the "imaginary forces" of the spectators sitting or standing before that same stage which in *As You Like It* passed muster as equivalent to "all the world."

> Still be kind
> And eke out our performance with your mind.

The performance must be eked out. It is only a substitute for the real glory of England, King Harry, and Agincourt.

And so our scene must to the battle fly,
Where—O for pity!—we shall much disgrace
With four or five most vile and ragged foils,
Right ill-dispos'd in brawl ridiculous,
The name of Agincourt.

Vouchsafe to those that have not read the story,
That I may prompt them; and of such as have,
I humbly pray them to admit the excuse
Of time, of numbers, and due course of things,
Which cannot in their huge and proper life
Be here presented.

Shakespeare never stops apologizing, even in his epilogue where he has such good reason to boast. At best it has been a play

In little room confining mighty men,
Mangling by starts the full course of their glory.

Precisely here is where the great movie of Laurence Olivier gets its inspiration. It is not to improve on Shakespeare, or make him more comprehensible, or say what he could not say. It is simply to show—and to the eye—what Shakespeare so clearly would have liked to show. It is to mount ships before us, to fill the Channel with them, to disembark them on the coast of France, to make visible the knights and bowmen who went forth from them to inhabit vasty fields, to reveal these men in all the extremities of peril, sickness, fear, wrath, and victory, to set them around their campfires, to make audible their horses in the night, to spread indeed the whole tapestry of successful war so that all men may stand and read its last detail. Furthermore it is to people the beautiful palaces of France—palaces which a colored screen can realize to the point that we who look on may imagine ourselves inside the best paintings of the fifteenth century—with brilliant soldiers and ladies, and to let the voice of one of those ladies, the Princess Katherine, be heard in the most intimate confidences. It is also to bring us close up—much closer than any stage could do—to the common soldiers of England who on the eve of Agincourt lie by their fires and wonder about the morals of even the justest war. The King is there incognito, speaking of his just cause and his honorable quarrel.

> *Williams.* That's more than we know. . . . If the cause be not good, the King himself hath a heavy reckoning to make, when all those legs and arms and heads, chopp'd off in a battle, shall join together at the latter day and cry all, "We died at such a place;" some swearing, some crying for a surgeon, some upon their wives left poor behind them, some upon the debts they owe, some upon their children rawly left. I am afeard there are few die well that die in a battle; for how can they charitably dispose of anything, when blood is their argument? Now, if these men do not die well, it will be a black matter for the King that led them to it.

The King has an answer to this too, but no person who has heard it will forget the question that was asked. And there is an undeniable advantage for both the poetry and the play in this power of the camera at such a moment to move directly up to the speaker, isolating him from all the world as he mutters out of the deepest part of his conscience.

Shakespeare's play is in truth a series of such moments. It is not so much a drama as a galaxy of bright dramatic fragments. That is how he saw his subject, and that perhaps is why he yearned for the effect of reality—each fragment, to exert its utmost power, should be experienced perfectly and apart, with every benefit from our ability to believe it as true, as immediately before us. The fragments are many and amazing. There are the rascals of the piece, for instance: the Pistol and the Bardolph of *Henry IV*, but with Nym now for good measure. And there is the incomparable Fluellen, the Welsh officer who fights out of the book of war. He is a fussy fellow, full of precedents and principles, and most of what he sees going on shocks him because it is not according to his Hoyle. The movie does him grand justice, even if it leaves his best words out. They come toward the end of his comparison between Harry and Alexander the Great. The two monarchs, he is saying, are like one another because they were both born on rivers, and because both of them turned away their best friends—in the one case Cleitus, in the other case Falstaff. But the immortal part of the speech has to do with the rivers. "There is salmons in both." Therefore are Harry and Alexander alike. It is the classic instance in all literature of the forced comparison. But the sentence is not spoken in the movie.

That it is not is only another reminder that plays and movies are different things. A play is to be heard and understood, a movie is to be seen. A movie made from a play, even one of Shakespeare's, will of necessity ignore many of its words, since words are not its medium. Laurence Olivier could not keep all of Shakespeare's words and still have the movie he wanted—or, as has been suggested, that Shakespeare himself wanted. Shakespeare for once was not content with words. He wanted pictures. And here, three centuries and a half later, he has them—may it be—to the content of his deathless heart.

MARK VAN DOREN

Introduction

THE emergence of the historical drama during the last decade of Elizabeth's reign, and the popularity which it achieved during its brief existence, were the natural outcome of the consciousness of national unity and national greatness to which England was then awakening. Haunted for more than a quarter of a century by the constant dread of foreign invasion and domestic treachery, the country could at last breathe freely, and the fervid patriotism which now animated every order in the State found appropriate expression in "a noble and solid curiosity" to learn the story of the nation's past. Of this curiosity the theatres, then as always the reflection of the popular taste, were not slow to take advantage. To the earlier Chronicle Plays succeeded the *Edward II.* of Marlowe, the *Edward I.* of Peele, and the anonymous play of *Edward III.;* the influence of Marlowe on his contemporaries was paramount, and it was under his banner that Shakespeare himself, who had entered the field with revisions of earlier plays on the wars of York and Lancaster, was content for a while to range himself. *Richard III.,* however, remained his solitary effort in Marlowesque, imitation was soon to give way to originality, and in *Richard II.* and *King John* he proved that he had now felt his strength, and had left his predecessors far behind. Nor was he destined to stop here; in 1597 he took up the thread of the story which he had dropped some three years earlier, and in the three greatest dramas that have ever been founded on the history of England, he set the crown upon his labours, and filled up the gap which had been left between the death of Richard II. and the accession of Henry VI. The popularity of these three plays was at once assured by

Introduction

an innovation, which in itself marks an epoch in the history of the drama. Taking the hint from an earlier play, of which we shall have more to say later, he grafted upon the serious portion of his subject a comedy of "humours," which was alone enough to make the fortune of a dramatic performance of far inferior merit. Such a favourite, indeed, was the leading "humorist" in these plays, that to judge from the numerous allusions to him in documents, literary and non-literary, of the seventeenth century, Falstaff shared with Hamlet the honour of being the best known creation of Shakespeare. As for the theatre-going public, they could never have enough of him, and we may suspect that it was partly with a view of soothing the indignation aroused by his unlooked-for humiliation at the hands of his former patron and ally, that the speaker of the epilogue to the Second Part of *Henry IV.* was allowed to promise his admirers a continuation of the story "with Sir John in it," and (another hint from the old play) to "make you merry with fair Katharine of France"—as if there *could* possibly be any need for any further attraction!

The way in which this promise was fulfilled was peculiar. Two plays appeared: in one of them the story *was* continued, and fair Katharine was there to make them merry; Sir John, however, was seen no more: in the other the story *was not* continued, but there was Sir John in his full proportions—at least so said the bills; the more critical spectators probably came away with a shrewd suspicion that they had been imposed upon.

Which of these two plays—*Henry V.* and *The Merry Wives of Windsor*—preceded the other is a question upon which the critics are still divided. . . .

Introduction

We must pass to Shakespeare's conception of the character of Henry, and its relation to the popular tradition. In the main his Henry is the Henry of popular tradition, as the Henry of popular tradition is in the main the Henry of history. In dealing with personages so remote, both in time and nationality, as Coriolanus or even Julius Cæsar, some sacrifice of historic truth at the shrine of dramatic effect might be excusable enough, but in painting the portrait of the national hero no such liberty would be either permissible or necessary. There was, however, one article in the popular belief, which, in its crudest form, could not but give pause to the reflective mind, and which the subtle analysis of the poet must necessarily modify or at least explain. No feature in the character of the national hero had seized a firmer hold on the imagination of his countrymen than his supposed miraculous conversion from the wild licence of the prince to the sober majesty of the king: not only was this conversion miraculous, but it was sudden:

> The breath no sooner left his father's body,
> But that his wildness, mortified in him,
> Seem'd to die too.

The two bishops (Act I. sc. i.) attempt with little success to explain the mystery. And if sudden, it was of course unexpected, even by his own brothers.

> Well you must now speak Sir John Falstaff fair,
> Which swims against your stream of quality,

says Clarence to the Chief Justice, now that the old king had "walk'd the way of nature." But the entrance of the new monarch soon shows him that he had been wrong in his calculations:

Introduction

My father is gone wild into his grave,
For in his tomb lie my affections;
And with his spirit sadly I survive,
To mock the expectation of the world,
To frustrate prophecies, and to raze out
Rotten opinion, who hath writ me down
After my seeming. The tide of blood in me
Hath proudly flow'd in vanity till now:
Now doth it turn and ebb back to the sea,
Where it shall mingle with the state of floods
And flow henceforth in formal majesty.

(2 Henry IV. v. ii.)

These words can leave no doubt of his conversion in the minds of those to whom they are addressed; the difficulty was to explain it. To the superficial observers it seemed miraculous and sudden: Shakespeare who looked beneath the surface thought otherwise. In his view if his brothers had known him better they would have been prepared for what took place: in his view explanations such as those attempted by the two bishops, or by Warwick,

The prince but studies his companions
Like a strange tongue, wherein, to gain the language,
'Tis needful that the most immodest word
Be look'd upon and learn'd,

(2 Henry IV. iv. iv. 68—71)

are beside the mark; in his view Henry is a man of unswerving purpose, a man who has his goal in view and marches steadily towards it—a character eminently consistent, and with a method even in its madness.

On our very first introduction to him (*1 Henry IV*. i. ii.) Shakespeare is careful to let us see that he has already realised the responsibilities of his position; already he has his ideal, and he means to act up to it. His soliloquy at the close of the scene lets us into the secret. It is not difficult to detect his consciousness of the danger of the inheritance to which he is destined to succeed: he has not failed to recognise that for him a throne will be no seat of luxury and ease; this must in fact have been the stern lesson of his early years, a lesson emphasised again in the two Parts of *Henry IV*. The note struck in the very first line of the former,

> So shaken as we are, so wan with care,

reverberates throughout to the last line of the latter. There is no peace for the usurper: conscious as he is of the "by-paths and indirect crook'd ways" by which he won the crown, and knowing well "how troublesome it sat upon his head" (*2 Henry IV*. IV. v.), yet in spite of all the attempts to wrest it from his grasp, he has never relaxed his hold, and though he may now bequeath it to his son with brighter hopes, yet secure possession is still distant,

> Yet, though thou stand'st more sure than I could do,
> Thou art not firm enough, since griefs are green.

There are still jealous rivals and discontented adherents, for whose restless activities a safer outlet must be provided, and his last legacy to his successor is one of war,

> Therefore, my Harry,
> Be it thy course to busy giddy minds
> With foreign quarrels; that action, hence borne out,
> May waste the memory of the former days.

Accordingly the play closes appropriately with Prince John of Lancaster's shrewd forecast of the future:

> I will lay odds, that, ere this year expire,
> We bear our civil swords and native fire
> As far as France: I heard a bird so sing,
> Whose music, to my thinking, pleas'd the king.
> (*2 Henry IV.* v. v.)

Introduction

We now return to the soliloquy. With this statesmanlike grasp of realities Henry combines a young man's love of excitement and frivolity. Whatever other people may think, and whatever he himself may say in a momentary fit of self-depreciation, he sees no irreconcilable discrepancy between the two: he will enjoy himself as long as the time allows, but whatever liberty he may permit himself for the present, there is one point on which he has finally decided, and that is that no mere enjoyment shall interfere with the serious business of life. Behind all his jesting and merriment in the company of Falstaff and his jovial crew, we are conscious of the presence of this resolve, a presence for the most part silent, but which now and then betrays itself in words. At the very first opportunity the Prince takes us into his confidence himself:

> I know you all, and will a while uphold
> The unyok'd humour of your idleness.

And then, after likening himself to the sun which shines forth all the more welcome to us after a period of obscurity he continues:

> So, when this loose behaviour I throw off,
> And pay the debt I never promised,
> By how much better than my word I am
> By so much shall I falsify men's hopes;
> And like bright metal on a sullen ground,
> My reformation, glittering o'er my fault,
> Shall show more goodly, and attract more eyes
> Than that which hath no foil to set it off.

I do not believe that these words are intended to be taken as a deliberate statement of any deliberate purpose with which he had entered upon "this loose behaviour"; I do not believe that he means that he is deliberately assuming the part of a scapegrace in order that he may afterwards turn his conduct to account, by means of the enhanced glory with which he will shine when the time comes for him to throw off the disguise. As Mr. Boswell-Stone observes, if he "was really influenced by such a motive, one . . . must condemn his aim as contemptible." Such a man "could not be expected to reach a heroic standard. His nature must be a radically false one, and his objects petty. We cannot suppose the hero of Shakespeare's drama, a king whose fame still lives among us, could ever reason thus." Granted, but when the same writer goes on to explain away the plain meaning of the lines as being merely "a salve for his conscience, a sophism to excuse his unwillingness to leave his joyous youth behind him, and turn, so early as the king would have him, to the wearisome duties of his station," I fear I cannot follow him. Such a theory would imply a capacity for self-deception, for being quieted with a "sophism," which appears to me to be foreign to Henry's character. If he can be acquitted of "deliberate calculations of vanity," I fear he cannot be acquitted of meaning what he says; and I would suggest that having affirmed his intention of continuing to enjoy for the present the society of the tavern, his practical nature instantly fastens upon the advantage which will incidentally result. His is pre-eminently a genius for success: his very extravagances shall *tell*; he set out on his career of wildness with no other thought than that of amusement, but once embarked on it he cannot and will not shut his eyes to the politic uses that may be made of it:

> I'll so offend to make offence a skill;
> Redeeming time when men think least I will.

There is no self-deception, no salving of conscience here; rather, to put it somewhat coarsely, a sturdy resolution to make the best of a bad business. The truth is there is no hesitancy or vacillation in Henry; that internal struggle which distracts the mind more finely touched than his, is unknown to his strenuous and masterful nature; he never bends under the weight of his responsibilities, nor does he ever fail to cope with facts: instead of the event shaping his character, his character seems to shape the event; he stands out, in short, from all the other heroes of Shakespeare as the man who knows what he wants to do, and who does it. That having once pictured to himself this incidental advantage arising from his present conduct he did not forget it, we have already seen in the words he uses upon his accession (*2 Henry IV*. v. ii.), where he tells us that he survives

> To mock the expectation of the world,

—the world which had writ him down after his seeming. Shakespeare, however, had writ him down otherwise, as we shall now endeavour to show.

Before they leave London to confront the rebels at Shrewsbury, the king has an interview with his son (*1 Henry IV*. III. ii.) in which he reproaches him with his evil courses, and compares him to Richard II., that skipping king, who mingled his royalty with capering fools, and grew a companion to the common streets. The Prince's apology is modest and dignified: his father has been misled by smiling pickthanks and base newsmongers; he will hereafter be more himself,

> And in the closing of some glorious day
> Be bold to tell you that I am your son.

And then follow the splendid lines in which he vows either to wash away his misdeeds in the blood of Hotspur, or perish in the attempt. Consistently in the next scene we find him busied with preparations for marching against the rebels:

> The land is burning; Percy stands on high;
> And either we or they must lower lie.

He cannot rest till he and Hotspur have met. When he overtakes Falstaff on the road to Shrewsbury it is, "Sirrah, make haste: Percy is already in the field" (*1 Henry IV.* IV. ii. 80). Then comes his generous tribute to his rival at the conference in the king's camp which preceded the fighting, the combat itself, and the Prince's triumph. And here we may remark as illustrating the comparative value which he attached to the serious and the lighter side of life, the contrast between the eloquent homage which he pays to the dead Percy, and the tone of half-amused, half-patronising regret in which he takes leave of the supposed dead Falstaff (V. iv. 102–110). In fact it is the humour of the situation which strikes him first:

> What! old acquaintance! could not all this flesh
> Keep in a little life?

The pathos, such as it is, comes afterwards,

> Poor Jack, farewell!
> I could have better spar'd a better man:

and then he even breaks into rhyme—a sure sign of the absence of any real depth of feeling. We pass over his chivalrous treatment of the captured Douglas, and in the next play, on his return from the overthrow of Glendower, we meet him once more in the company of Poins (2 *Henry IV*. II. ii.). His father lies upon a sickbed, and if he does not outwardly manifest his grief, it is only because Poins and those like him would accuse him of hypocrisy: "thou thinkest me," he says, "as far in the devil's book as thou and Falstaff for obduracy and persistency; *let the end try the man*." Meantime he will once more visit his old haunts, and entertain himself with the humour of his old associate, but it is for the last time: in the midst of all the merriment appears the writing on the wall; twenty weak and weary posts come hurrying from the north; the serious business of life claims all his energies, and the chapter of his frivolities is soon to close for ever:

> By heaven, Poins, I feel me much to blame,
> So idly to profane the precious time,
> When tempest of commotion, like the south,
> Borne with black vapour, doth begin to melt,
> And drop upon our bare unarmed heads.
> Give me my sword and cloak. Falstaff, good night.
>
> (II. iv. 390–395.)

We are left to conjecture that it is his father's illness which prevents him from taking the field in person against the northern lords. Had he been present, we may be sure that the stupendous act of treachery by which his brother gets them into his power would never have stained the annals of his house. The old king still sees only the apparent levity of his son's character, and is full of gloomy anticipations of the time, now not far distant, when

> the fifth Harry from curb'd license plucks
> The muzzle of restraint;

not until his last moments does he recognise the sterling worth that lies beneath the surface. The Prince convinces him at last of his loyalty and affection:

If I do feign,
O! let me in my present wildness die
And never live to show the incredulous world
The noble change that I have purposed!

(IV. v. 152–155.)

He has held firmly to his resolution of redeeming the time; we have already seen it emphasised on his accession, and I think we ought now to be prepared for its fulfilment. It is true that it is impossible to read the famous scene with which the play closes (V. v.) without a shock, without a certain feeling of resentment: the personal lecture which the newly crowned monarch thinks fit to deliver to his old boon companion we may think ill-timed and ill-judged, his committal to the Fleet unjust; we may say with Hostess Quickly that "The king has killed his heart," and with Ancient Pistol that "His heart is fracted and corroborate"; but shocked and indignant as we may be, I submit that if the view of Henry's character which I have tried to indicate is correct, we have no right to feel surprised; or if surprised, our surprise should be reserved for the lecture and the imprisonment; the curt dismissal of Falstaff and all his crew is the climax to which the undercurrent of events has all along been tending.

The above excursion through the two earlier plays has been necessary in order to bring out Shakespeare's conception of a genuine consistency in Henry's character underlying the apparent miracle of a sudden conversion. In the present play there are no inconsistencies to detain us; his character is no longer in the making—it is made. Conscientious, brave, just, capable, and tenacious, Henry stands before us as the embodiment of worldly success, and as such he is entitled to our unreserved admiration. It would be an insult to the intelligence of the reader to insist further on the details of a char-

Introduction

acter which every line of the play enables him to realise for himself. Such a character he will accept with its inseparable limitations, as Shakespeare intended it to be accepted; he will not look for those finer touches of the intellect or of the emotions which mark the hero of another sort; he will miss, as has been well said, the light that is upon the brow of a Hamlet or an Othello; he will not find a man of whom it can be said,

> a rarer spirit never
> Did steer humanity—

but he *will* find a true ruler of men, a man no pipe for fortune's finger, a man at all times master of his fate, a man who, once satisfied of the justice of his end, swerved neither to the right hand nor to the left till he had achieved it.

A word must be said on the conduct of the action. So much has been written on the exceptional character of this play, that it is not necessary to labour the point here. As has been so often pointed out, its interest is epic rather than dramatic; it is the nearest approach on the part of the author to a national epic. His aim is above everything patriotic; his audience, even in spite of themselves, shall be compelled to recognise the greatness of their country's destiny, and to this end no resource that the poet can command shall be spared:

> O! for a Muse of fire, that would ascend
> The brightest heaven of invention!

In no play is the strenuousness of poetic effort more conspicuous, or the flow of impassioned rhetoric more sustained. To this end again he has no need of skilfully constructed plot, or subtle analysis of character; but in a succession of highly elaborate and highly realistic pictures the national hero, that mirror of all Christian kings, shall stand before the eyes of the spectators in his very habit as he lived. This persistent realism also explains the introduction of the Chorus: it may serve to mark the division between the Acts, to bridge over the intervals of time, and even to apologise for the inadequacy of the stage appliances;—it may do all this and yet not justify its existence; all these demands are made in other plays where there is no Chorus to satisfy them; the peculiar function of the Chorus in *Henry V.* is the appeal it makes to the historic imagination. The success or failure of the piece depends in a more than ordinary degree upon the extent to which the spectator can be made by means of the mimic shows of things to visualise the actual events for which they stand: the tension must never be relaxed, the eye of the mind must be as active as the eye of the body: the fervid appeals have sometimes almost the accent of despair:

> Follow, follow!
> Grapple your minds to sternage of this navy.

Again—

> Work, work your thoughts, and therein see a siege;
> Behold the ordnance on their carriages,
> *With fatal mouths gaping on girded Harfleur.*

And again—

> But now behold
> In the quick forge and working-house of thought. . .

In a modern representation, such as it has been my lot to witness, with these sonorous and majestic incantations left out, the play loses half its justification, half its real charm.

But epic as is the main impression produced by the play, it is not for all that exempt from the ordinary laws of dramatic action: the connecting plot is there, though we are apt to lose sight of it in the splendour of the situations that it links together. Thus in Act I. the causes of the action are set forth: in Act II. and the earlier scenes of Act III., its triumph over the obstacles that would have checked its growth, and its gradual progress towards the climax. This is reached in the enfeebled and famished condition to which the English army is reduced on its march to Calais (III. v. 56–60, and vi. 145–164).

Everything now depends upon the result of a single engagement; and for a while we are held in suspense, but the dénouement follows in the victory of the English, and the subsequent alliance between the two countries. The comic scenes have an interest of their own, and in no way affect the course of the main action; as Mr. Boswell-Stone observes, they "serve merely to vary the sameness of the historical action, and give more reality to the events by associating them with ordinary human interests and people."

Another question remains which we must not pass over without notice. Some critics have imagined that in writing this play Shakespeare had an eye to the events of his own day, and intended by the way to convey a political lesson. This view was first put forward by Mr. Richard Simpson in his paper on the "Politics of Shakspere's Historical Plays": in the play of *Henry V.* he finds a pronouncement in favour of the party of Essex: the acts of Essex "uniformly point to a grand idea of a union of all parties and all nationalities which were to be found in our group of Islands. This involved equal justice to all, a general toleration in religion, and an abolition of the privileges of one sect and of the penalties attached to another." To secure these ends he advocated a policy of foreign war; war abroad was the one salve for civil and religious dissensions at home. "Such is the policy of *Henry V*. It is a poem of victory, a glorification of war, not as an agony of brutal passions, but as an agent of civilisation—'when lenity and cruelty play for a kingdom, the gentler gamester is the soonest winner'" (III. vi. 116). For these ends also he favoured the succession of James to the English throne, and at the close of the play we have only to substitute "Scotland" for "France" to make the lesson plain; "the play ends with the union of the two belligerent countries, a symbol of the coming union with Scotland, and with the prayer—God combine your realms in one! may it be a spousal of the kingdoms, that no jealousy may thrust in between their paction."

Of the value of this kind of interpretation I leave the reader to judge; personally, I think it dangerous, as tending to prove more than is warranted by the evidence: to say that a political lesson may be drawn from a work of dramatic art is one thing, to say that the author created it with the view of conveying such lesson is another; nor does it follow that because a great poet may, broadly speaking, have a moral purpose, he would ever hamper it by such limitations of time and place as the word "political" implies.

As a case in point to support his contention that union between the four nationalities of these islands is advocated, Mr. Simpson appeals to Act III. sc. ii., where the Welsh, English, Scottish, and Irish captains are introduced serving side by side under a common flag, "as if to symbolise the union of the four nations under one crown, and their co-operation in enterprises of honour, no longer hindered by the touchiness of a separate nationalism." It has further been suggested that the latter part of this scene, in which the Irishman and the Scotsman appear, is a later insertion; this seems probable, but I think the insertion, if such it be, may be explained on other grounds than those indicated by Mr. Simpson. The facts regarding this part of the scene are some-what peculiar. Gower brings a message from the Duke of Gloucester requiring Fluellen's immediate attendance at the mines; instead of obeying orders, Fluellen begins to criticise the engineering as "not according to the disciplines of the war," and this leads Gower to mention that the work is directed by a valiant Irishman—one Captain Macmorris, as Fluellen appears to be aware. True to the proverb, Macmorris then makes his appearance, "and the Scots captain, Captain Jamy, with him." This is the only appearance on the stage of this pair of worthies, and it is remarkable that from this point to the end of the scene the abbreviation prefixed to Fluellen's speeches suddenly becomes *Welch.* in the Folio instead of *Flu.* as uniformly hitherto and afterwards; quite consistently Jamy and Macmorris are distinguished as *Scot.* and *Irish.* Thus the Welshman, the Scotsman, and the Irishman, with a word or two from the Englishman, Gower, have the rest of the scene to themselves, and we are entertained with a violent altercation between Fluellen and Macmorris, while Jamy is too canny to do more than express his interest in the dispute without taking sides with either party.

Now it will not be denied that all this is an excrescence upon the rest of the scene; the only doubt is how to account for it. In any case it has all the appearance of an afterthought; the very gratuitous and isolated intrusion of the Scottish and Irish captains serves no dramatic purpose, except so far as it gives greater scope to the part of the Welshman; it gives him one more chance of a disputation touching the disciplines of the war. But I very much doubt whether this addition was made with any idea of symbolising the union of the component parts of the United Kingdom. I would suggest a less ambitious motive. Fluellen had been a great success, his countryman Sir Hugh had secured the honour of special mention on the title-page of the Quarto of the play in which he figures, the "variable and pleasing humors" of the two Welshmen had brought down the house: "You have done so well with Taffy," we may imagine someone saying to the stage-manager, I will not say the author, "let us see what you can make of Paddy and Sandy." Hence the added portion, and hence the writer of it, whoever he may have been, to balance *Scot.* and *Irish.* is fain to dub Fluellen *Welch*. The two former having answered their purpose disappear into obscurity from which they emerged.

ABOUT THE TEXT

The reader is requested to note that the text of the present edition is substantially that of the Folio of 1623, modernised as far as spelling and punctuation are concerned.

DRAMATIS PERSONÆ

KING HENRY THE FIFTH.
DUKE OF GLOUCESTER, }
DUKE OF BEDFORD, } *Brothers to the King.*
DUKE OF EXETER, *Uncle to the King.*
DUKE OF YORK, *Cousin to the King.*
EARLS OF SALISBURY, WESTMORELAND, *and* WARWICK.
ARCHBISHOP OF CANTERBURY.   BISHOP OF ELY.
EARL OF CAMBRIDGE.   LORD SCROOP.   SIR THOMAS GREY.
SIR THOMAS ERPINGHAM, GOWER, FLUELLEN, MACMORRIS,
    JAMY, *Officers in King Henry's Army.*
BATES, COURT, WILLIAMS, *Soldiers in the same.*
PISTOL, NYM, BARDOLPH.   *Boy.   A Herald.*

CHARLES THE SIXTH, *King of France.*
LEWIS, *the Dauphin.*
DUKES OF BURGUNDY, ORLEANS, *and* BOURBON.
The Constable of France.   Governor of Harfleur.
RAMBURES *and* GRANDPRE, *French Lords.*
MONTJOY, *a French Herald.*
Ambassadors to the King of England.

ISABEL, *Queen of France.*
KATHARINE, *Daughter to Charles and Isabel.*
ALICE, *A Lady attending on the Princess.*
*Hostess of a tavern in Eastcheap, formerly Mistress Quickly, and
    now married to Pistol.*

*Lords, Ladies, Officers, French and English Soldiers, Citizens,
    Messengers, and Attendants.*

WILLIAM SHAKESPEARE:

The Life of King Henry the Fifth

"O! for a Muse of fire, that would ascend
The brightest heaven of invention"

The Life of Henry the Fifth

O! for a Muse of fire, that would ascend
The brightest heaven of invention;
A kingdom for a stage, princes to act
And monarchs to behold the swelling scene.
Then should the warlike Harry, like himself,
Assume the port of Mars; and at his heels,
Leash'd in like hounds, should famine, sword, and fire
Crouch for employment. But pardon, gentles all,
The flat unraised spirits that hath dar'd
On this unworthy scaffold to bring forth
So great an object: can this cockpit hold
The vasty fields of France? or may we cram
Within this wooden O the very casques
That did affright the air at Agincourt?
O, pardon! since a crooked figure may
Attest in little place a million;
And let us, ciphers to this great accompt,
On your imaginary forces work.
Suppose within the girdle of these walls
Are now confin'd two mighty monarchies,
Whose high upreared and abutting fronts
The perilous narrow ocean parts asunder:
Piece out our imperfections with your thoughts;
Into a thousand parts divide one man,

And make imaginary puissance;
Think, when we talk of horses, that you see them
Printing their proud hoofs i' the receiving earth;
For 'tis your thoughts that now must deck our kings,
Carry them here and there, jumping o'er times,
Turning the accomplishment of many years
Into an hour-glass: for the which supply,
Admit me Chorus to this history;
Who prologue-like your humble patience pray,
Gently to hear, kindly to judge, our play.   [*Exit.*

ACT I

SCENE I.—*London. An Antechamber in the King's Palace.*

Enter the Archbishop of CANTERBURY *and the Bishop of* ELY.

Cant.   My lord, I'll tell you; that self bill is urg'd,
      Which in the eleventh year of the last king's reign
      Was like, and had indeed against us pass'd,
      But that the scambling and unquiet time
      Did push it out of farther question.
Ely.   But how, my lord, shall we resist it now?
Cant.   It must be thought on. If it pass against us,
      We lose the better half of our possession;
      For all the temporal lands which men devout
      By testament have given to the church
      Would they strip from us; being valued thus:
      As much as would maintain, to the king's honour,
      Full fifteen earls and fifteen hundred knights,
      Six thousand and two hundred good esquires;

And, to relief of lazars and weak age,
Of indigent faint souls past corporal toil,
A hundred almshouses right well supplied;
And to the coffers of the king beside,
A thousand pounds by the year. Thus runs the bill.

Ely.   This would drink deep.

Cant.   'Twould drink the cup and all.

Ely.   But what prevention?

Cant.   The king is full of grace and fair regard.

Ely.   And a true lover of the holy church.

Cant.   The courses of his youth promis'd it not.
The breath no sooner left his father's body,
But that his wildness, mortified in him,
Seem'd to die too; yea, at that very moment,
Consideration like an angel came,
And whipp'd the offending Adam out of him,
Leaving his body as a paradise,
To envelop and contain celestial spirits.
Never was such a sudden scholar made;
Never came reformation in a flood,
With such a heady currance, scouring faults;
Nor never Hydra-headed wilfulness
So soon did lose his seat and all at once
As in this king.

Ely.   We are blessed in the change.

Cant.   Hear him but reason in divinity,
And, all-admiring, with an inward wish
You would desire the king were made a prelate:
Hear him debate of commonwealth affairs,
You would say it hath been all in all his study:
List his discourse of war, and you shall hear

A fearful battle render'd you in music:
Turn him to any cause of policy,
The Gordian knot of it he will unloose,
Familiar as his garter; that, when he speaks,
The air, a charter'd libertine, is still,
And the mute wonder lurketh in men's ears,
To steal his sweet and honey'd sentences;
So that the art and practic part of life
Must be the mistress to this theoric:
Which is a wonder how his grace should glean it,
Since his addiction was to courses vain;
His companies unletter'd, rude, and shallow;
His hours fill'd up with riots, banquets, sports;
And never noted in him any study,
Any retirement, any sequestration
From open haunts and popularity.

Ely.   The strawberry grows underneath the nettle,
And wholesome berries thrive and ripen best
Neighbour'd by fruit of baser quality:
And so the prince obscur'd his contemplation
Under the veil of wildness; which, no doubt,
Grew like the summer grass, fastest by night,
Unseen, yet crescive in his faculty.

Cant.   It must be so; for miracles are ceas'd;
And therefore we must needs admit the means
How things are perfected.

Ely.   But, my good lord,
How now for mitigation of this bill
Urg'd by the commons? Doth his majesty
Incline to it, or no?

Cant.   He seems indifferent,

Or rather swaying more upon our part
Than cherishing the exhibiters against us;
For I have made an offer to his majesty,
Upon our spiritual convocation,
And in regard of causes now in hand,
Which I have open'd to his grace at large,
As touching France, to give a greater sum
Than ever at one time the clergy yet
Did to his predecessors part withal.

Ely.   How did this offer seem receiv'd, my lord?

Cant.   With good acceptance of his majesty;
Save that there was not time enough to hear,
As I perceiv'd his grace would fain have done,
The severals and unhidden passages
Of his true titles to some certain dukedoms,
And generally to the crown and seat of France,
Deriv'd from Edward, his great-grandfather.

Ely.   What was the impediment that broke this off?

Cant.   The French ambassador upon that instant
Crav'd audience; and the hour I think is come
To give him hearing: is it four o'clock?

Ely.   It is.

Cant.   Then go we in to know his embassy;
Which I could with a ready guess declare
Before the Frenchman speak a word of it.

Ely.   I'll wait upon you, and I long to hear it.   [*Exeunt*

SCENE II.—*The Same. The Presence Chamber.*

Enter KING HENRY, GLOUCESTER, BEDFORD, EXETER,
WARWICK, WESTMORELAND, *and Attendants.*

K. Hen.   Where is my gracious lord of Canterbury?
Exe.   Not here in presence.
K. Hen.   Send for him, good uncle.
West.   Shall we call in the ambassador, my liege?
K. Hen.   Not yet, my cousin: we would be resolv'd,
Before we hear him, of some things of weight
That task our thoughts, concerning us and France.

Enter the Archbishop of CANTERBURY *and the Bishop of* ELY.

Cant.   God and his angels guard your sacred throne,
And make you long become it!
K. Hen.   Sure, we thank you.
My learned lord, we pray you to proceed,
And justly and religiously unfold
Why the law Salique that they have in France
Or should, or should not, bar us in our claim.
And God forbid, my dear and faithful lord,
That you should fashion, wrest, or bow your reading,
Or nicely charge your understanding soul
With opening titles miscreate, whose right
Suits not in native colours with the truth;
For God doth know how many now in health
Shall drop their blood in approbation
Of what your reverence shall incite us to.
Therefore take heed how you impawn our person,
How you awake our sleeping sword of war:
We charge you, in the name of God, take heed;

"*Consideration like an angel came,*
And whipp'd the offending Adam out of him"

For never two such kingdoms did contend
Without much fall of blood; whose guiltless drops
Are every one a woe, a sore complaint
'Gainst him whose wrongs give edge unto the swords
That make such waste in brief mortality.
Under this conjuration speak, my lord,
And we will hear, note, and believe in heart
That what you speak is in your conscience wash'd
As pure as sin with baptism.

Cant.　Then hear me, gracious sovereign, and you peers,
That owe yourselves, your lives, and services
To this imperial throne. There is no bar
To make your highness' claim to France
But this, which they produce from Pharamond,
In terram Salicam mulieres ne succedant,
"No woman shall succeed in Salique land":
Which Salique land the French unjustly gloze
To be the realm of France, and Pharamond
The founder of this law and female bar.
Yet their own authors faithfully affirm
That the land Salique is in Germany,
Between the floods of Sala and of Elbe;
Where Charles the Great having subdued the Saxons—
There left behind and settled certain French;
Who, holding in disdain the German women
For some dishonest manners of their life,
Establish'd then this law; to wit, no female
Should be inheritrix in Salique land:
Which Salique, as I said, 'twixt Elbe and Sala,
Is at this day in Germany call'd Meisen.
Then doth it well appear the Salique law

Was not devised for the realm of France;
Nor did the French possess the Salique land
Until four hundred one and twenty years
After defunction of King Pharamond,
Idly suppos'd the founder of this law;
Who died within the year of our redemption
Four hundred twenty-six; and Charles the Great
Subdued the Saxons, and did seat the French
Beyond the river Sala, in the year
Eight hundred five. Besides, their writers say,
King Pepin, which deposed Childeric,
Did, as heir general, being descended
Of Blithild, which was daughter to King Clothair,
Make claim and title to the crown of France.
Hugh Capet also, who usurp'd the crown
Of Charles the Duke of Lorraine, sole heir male
Of the true line and stock of Charles the Great,
To find his title with some shows of truth,
Though, in pure truth, it was corrupt and naught,
Convey'd himself as heir to the Lady Lingare,
Daughter to Charlemain, who was the son
To Lewis the emperor, and Lewis the son
Of Charles the Great. Also King Lewis the Tenth,
Who was sole heir to the usurper Capet,
Could not keep quiet in his conscience,
Wearing the crown of France, till satisfied
That fair Queen Isabel, his grandmother,
Was lineal of the Lady Ermengare,
Daughter to Charles the aforesaid Duke of Lorraine:
By the which marriage the line of Charles the Great
Was re-united to the crown of France.

So that, as clear as is the summer's sun,
King Pepin's title, and Hugh Capet's claim,
King Lewis his satisfaction, all appear
To hold in right and title of the female:
So do the kings of France unto this day;
Howbeit they would hold up this Salique law
To bar your highness claiming from the female;
And rather choose to hide them in a net
Than amply to imbar their crooked titles
Usurp'd from you and your progenitors.

K. Hen.   May I with right and conscience make this claim?

Cant.   The sin upon my head, dread sovereign!
For in the book of Numbers is it writ:
"When the man dies, let the inheritance
Descend unto the daughter." Gracious lord,
Stand for your own; unwind your bloody flag;
Look back into your mighty ancestors:
Go, my dread lord, to your great-grandsire's tomb,
From whom you claim; invoke his war-like spirit,
And your great-uncle's, Edward the Black Prince,
Who on the French ground play'd a tragedy,
Making defeat on the full power of France;
Whiles his most mighty father on a hill
Stood smiling to behold his lion's whelp
Forage in blood of French nobility.
O noble English! that could entertain
With half their forces the full pride of France,
And let another half stand laughing by,
All out of work, and cold for action.

Ely.   Awake remembrance of these valiant dead,
And with your puissant arm renew their feats:

You are their heir, you sit upon their throne,
The blood and courage that renowned them
Runs in your veins; and my thrice-puissant liege
Is in the very May-morn of his youth,
Ripe for exploits and mighty enterprises.

Exe. Your brother kings and monarchs of the earth
Do all expect that you should rouse yourself,
As did the former lions of your blood.

West. They know your grace hath cause and means and
might;
So hath your highness; never king of England
Had nobles richer, and more loyal subjects,
Whose hearts have left their bodies here in England
And lie pavilion'd in the fields of France.

Cant. O! let their bodies follow, my dear liege,
With blood and sword and fire to win your right;
In aid whereof we of the spiritualty
Will raise your highness such a mighty sum
As never did the clergy at one time
Bring in to any of your ancestors.

K. Hen. We must not only arm to invade the French,
But lay down our proportions to defend
Against the Scot, who will make road upon us
With all advantages.

Cant. They of those marches, gracious sovereign,
Shall be a wall sufficient to defend
Our inland from the pilfering borderers.

K. Hen. We do not mean the coursing snatchers only,
But fear the main intendment of the Scot,
Who hath been still a giddy neighbour to us;
For you shall read that my great-grandfather

*"For never two such kingdoms did contend
Without much fall of blood"*

Never went with his forces into France
But that the Scot on his unfurnish'd kingdom
Came pouring, like the tide into a breach,
With ample and brim fulness of his force,
Galling the gleaned land with hot assays,
Girding with grievous siege castles and towns;
That England, being empty of defence,
Hath shook and trembled at the ill neighbourhood.

Cant.   She hath been then more fear'd than harm'd, my liege;
For hear her but exampled by herself:
When all her chivalry hath been in France
And she a mourning widow of her nobles,
She hath herself not only well defended,
But taken and impounded as a stray
The King of Scots; whom she did send to France,
To fill King Edward's fame with prisoner kings,
And make her chronicle as rich with praise
As is the ooze and bottom of the sea
With sunken wrack and sumless treasuries.

West.   But there's a saying very old and true;
    If that you will France win,
    Then with Scotland first begin:
For once the eagle England being in prey,
To her unguarded nest the weasel Scot
Comes sneaking and so sucks her princely eggs,
Playing the mouse in absence of the cat,
To tear and havoc more than she can eat.

Exe.   It follows then the cat must stay at home:
Yet that is but a crush'd necessity,
Since we have locks to safeguard necessaries
And pretty traps to catch the petty thieves.

While that the armed hand doth fight abroad
The advised head defends itself at home:
For government, though high and low and lower,
Put into parts, doth keep in one consent,
Congreeing in a full and natural close,
Like music.

Cant.   Therefore doth heaven divide
The state of man in divers functions,
Setting endeavour in continual motion;
To which is fixed, as an aim or butt,
Obedience: for so work the honey-bees,
Creatures that by a rule in nature teach
The act of order to a peopled kingdom.
They have a king and officers of sorts;
Where some, like magistrates, correct at home,
Others, like merchants, venture trade abroad,
Others, like soldiers, armed in their stings,
Make boot upon the summer's velvet buds;
Which pillage they with merry march bring home
To the tent-royal of their emperor:
Who, busied in his majesty, surveys
The singing masons building roofs of gold,
The civil citizens kneading up the honey,
The poor mechanic porters crowding in
Their heavy burdens at his narrow gate,
The sad-ey'd justice, with his surly hum,
Delivering o'er to executors pale
The lazy yawning drone. I this infer,
That many things, having full reference
To one consent, may work contrariously;
As many arrows, loosed several ways,

Come to one mark; as many ways meet in one town;
As many fresh streams meet in one salt sea;
As many lines close in the dial's centre;
So may a thousand actions, once afoot,
End in one purpose, and be all well borne
Without defeat. Therefore to France, my liege.
Divide your happy England into four;
Whereof take you one quarter into France,
And you withal shall make all Gallia shake.
If we, with thrice such powers left at home,
Cannot defend our own doors from the dog,
Let us be worried and our nation lose
The name of hardiness and policy.

K. Hen. Call in the messengers sent from the Dauphin.
                    [*Exeunt some Attendants.*

Now are we well resolv'd; and by God's help,
And yours, the noble sinews of our power,
France being ours, we'll bend it to our awe
Or break it all to pieces: or there we'll sit,
Ruling in large and ample empery
O'er France and all her almost kingly dukedoms,
Or lay these bones in an unworthy urn,
Tombless, with no remembrance over them:
Either our history shall with full mouth
Speak freely of our acts, or else our grave,
Like Turkish mute, shall have a tongueless mouth,
Not worshipp'd with a waxen epitaph.
                    Enter Ambassadors of France.
Now are we well prepar'd to know the pleasure
Of our fair cousin Dauphin; for we hear
Your greeting is from him, not from the king.

First Amb.   May't please your majesty to give us leave
    Freely to render what we have in charge;
    Or shall we sparingly show you far off
    The Dauphin's meaning and our embassy?

K. Hen.   We are no tyrant, but a Christian king;
    Unto whose grace our passion is as subject
    As are our wretches fetter'd in our prisons:
    Therefore with frank and with uncurbed plainness
    Tell us the Dauphin's mind.

First Amb.   Thus then, in few.
    Your highness, lately sending into France,
    Did claim some certain dukedoms, in the right
    Of your great predecessor, King Edward the Third.
    In answer of which claim, the prince our master
    Says that you savour too much of your youth,
    And bids you be advis'd: there's nought in France
    That can be with a nimble galliard won;
    You cannot revel into dukedoms there.
    He therefore sends you, meeter for your spirit,
    This tun of treasure; and, in lieu of this,
    Desires you let the dukedoms that you claim
    Hear no more of you. This the Dauphin speaks.

K. Hen.   What treasure, uncle?

Exe.   Tennis-balls, my liege.

K. Hen.   We are glad the Dauphin is so pleasant with us;
    His present and your pains we thank you for:
    When we have match'd our rackets to these balls,
    We will in France, by God's grace, play a set
    Shall strike his father's crown into the hazard.
    Tell him he hath made a match with such a wrangler
    That all the courts of France will be disturb'd

With chases. And we understand him well,
How he comes o'er us with our wilder days,
Not measuring what use we made of them.
We never valu'd this poor seat of England;
And therefore, living hence, did give ourself
To barbarous license; as 'tis ever common
That men are merriest when they are from home.
But tell the Dauphin I will keep my state,
Be like a king and show my sail of greatness
When I do rouse me in my throne of France:
For that I have laid by my majesty
And plodded like a man for working-days,
But I will rise there with so full a glory
That I will dazzle all the eyes of France,
Yea, strike the Dauphin blind to look on us.
And tell the pleasant prince this mock of his
Hath turn'd his balls to gun-stones; and his soul
Shall stand sore charged for the wasteful vengeance
That shall fly with them: for many a thousand widows
Shall this his mock mock out of their dear husbands;
Mock mothers from their sons, mock castles down;
And some are yet ungotten and unborn
That shall have cause to curse the Dauphin's scorn.
But this lies all within the will of God,
To whom I do appeal; and in whose name
Tell you the Dauphin I am coming on,
To venge me as I may and to put forth
My rightful hand in a well-hallow'd cause.
So get you hence in peace; and tell the Dauphin
His jest will savour but of shallow wit
When thousands weep more than did laugh at it.

Convey them with safe conduct. Fare you well.

[Exeunt Ambassadors.

Exe.   This was a merry message.

K. Hen.   We hope to make the sender blush at it.
Therefore, my lords, omit no happy hour
That may give furtherance to our expedition;
For we have now no thought in us but France,
Save those to God, that run before our business.
Therefore let our proportions for these wars
Be soon collected, and all things thought upon
That may with reasonable swiftness add
More feathers to our wings; for, God before,
We'll chide this Dauphin at his father's door.
Therefore let every man now task his thought,
That this fair action may on foot be brought.

[Exeunt. Flourish.

ACT II

Enter CHORUS.

Now all the youth of England are on fire,
And silken dalliance in the wardrobe lies;
Now thrive the armourers, and honour's thought
Reigns solely in the breast of every man:
They sell the pasture now to buy the horse,
Following the mirror of all Christian kings,
With winged heels, as English Mercuries.
For now sits Expectation in the air,
And hides a sword from hilts unto the point
With crowns imperial, crowns and coronets,
Promised to Harry and his followers.
The French, advis'd by good intelligence

"*When we have match'd our rackets to these balls,*
We will in France, by God's grace, play a set"

Of this most dreadful preparation,
Shake in their fear, and with pale policy
Seek to divert the English purposes.
O England! model to thy inward greatness,
Like little body with a mighty heart,
What might'st thou do, that honour would thee do,
Were all thy children kind and natural!
But see, thy fault France hath in thee found out,
A nest of hollow bosoms, which he fills
With treacherous crowns; and three corrupted men,
One, Richard Earl of Cambridge, and the second,
Henry Lord Scroop of Masham, and the third,
Sir Thomas Grey, knight, of Northumberland,
Have, for the gilt of France—O guilt indeed!—
Confirm'd conspiracy with fearful France;
And by their hands this grace of kings must die,
If hell and treason hold their promises,
Ere he takes ship for France, and in Southampton.
Linger your patience on; and we'll digest
The abuse of distance; force a play.
The sum is paid; the traitors are agreed;
The king is set from London; and the scene
Is now transported, gentles, to Southampton:
There is the playhouse now, there must you sit:
And thence to France shall we convey you safe,
And bring you back, charming the narrow seas
To give you gentle pass; for if we may,
We'll not offend one stomach with our play.
But, till the king come forth and not till then,
Unto Southampton do we shift our scene.   [*Exit.*

SCENE I.—*London. A Street.*

Enter CORPORAL NYM *and* LIEUTENANT BARDOLPH.

Bard. Well met, Corporal Nym.

Nym. Good morrow, Lieutenant Bardolph.

Bard. What, are Ancient Pistol and you friends yet?

Nym. For my part, I care not: I say little; but when time shall serve there shall be smiles; but that shall be as it may. I dare not fight; but I will wink and hold out mine iron. It is a simple one; but what though? it will toast cheese, and it will endure cold as another man's sword will: and there's an end.

Bard. I will bestow a breakfast to make you friends, and we'll be all three sworn brothers to France: let it be so, Good Corporal Nym.

Nym. Faith, I will live so long as I may, that's the certain of it; and when I cannot live any longer, I will do as I may: that is my rest, that is the rendezvous of it.

Bard. It is certain, corporal, that he is married to Nell Quickly; and certainly she did you wrong, for you were troth-plight to her.

Nym. I cannot tell; things must be as they may: men may sleep, and they may have their throats about them at that time; and some say knives have edges. It must be as it may: though patience be a tired mare, yet she will plod. There must be conclusions. Well, I cannot tell.

Enter PISTOL *and Hostess.*

Bard. Here comes Ancient Pistol and his wife. Good corporal, be patient here. How now, mine host Pistol!

Pist. Base tike, call'st thou me host?

Now, by this hand I swear, I scorn the term;

Nor shall my Nell keep lodgers.

Host.   No, by my troth, not long; for we cannot lodge and
 board a dozen or fourteen gentlewomen that live hon-
 estly by the prick of their needles, but it will be thought
 we keep a bawdy-house straight.

                                    [*Nym and Pistol draw.*
 O well-a-day, Lady, if he be not drawn now! we shall
 see wilful adultery and murder committed.

Bard.   Good lieutenant! good corporal! offer nothing here.

Nym.   Pish!

Pistol.   Pish for thee, Iceland dog! thou prick-ear'd cur of
 Iceland!

Host.   Good Corporal Nym, show thy valour and put
 up your sword.

Nym.   Will you shog off? I would have you solus.

Pist.   "Solus," egregious dog? O viper vile!
 The "solus" in thy most mervailous face;
 The "solus" in thy teeth, and in thy throat,
 And in thy hateful lungs, yea, in thy maw, perdy;
 And, which is worse, within thy nasty mouth!
 I do retort the "solus" in thy bowels;
 For I can take, and Pistol's cock is up,
 And flashing fire will follow.

Nym.   I am not Barbason; you cannot conjure me. I have
 an humour to knock you indifferently well. If you grow
 foul with me, Pistol, I will scour you with my rapier, as
 I may, in fair terms: if you would walk off, I would prick
 your guts a little, in good terms, as I may; and that's the
 humour of it.

Pist.   O braggard vile and damned furious wight!
 The grave doth gape, and doting death is near;

Therefore exhale.

Bard. Hear me, hear me what I say: he that strikes the first
stroke, I'll run him up to the hilts, as I am a soldier.

[*Draws.*

Pist. An oath of mickle might; and fury shall abate.
Give me thy fist, thy fore-foot to me give;
Thy spirits are most tall.

Nym. I will cut thy throat, one time or other, in fair terms;
that is the humour of it.

Pist. "Couple a gorge!"
That is the word. I thee defy again.
O hound of Crete, think'st thou my spouse to get?
No; to the spital go,
And from the powdering-tub of infamy
Fetch forth the lazar kite of Cressid's kind,
Doll Tearsheet she by name, and her espouse:
I have, and I will hold, the quondam Quickly
For the only she; and—pauca, there's enough.
Go to.

Enter the Boy.

Boy. Mine host Pistol, you must come to my master, and
your hostess: he is very sick, and would to bed. Good
Bardolph, put thy face between his sheets and do the
office of a warming-pan. Faith, he's very ill.

Bard. Away, you rogue!

Host. By my troth, he'll yield the crow a pudding one of
these days. The king has killed his heart. Good husband,
come home presently.   [*Exeunt Hostess and boy.*

Bard. Come, shall I make you two friends? We must to
France together. Why the devil should we keep knives
to cut one another's throats?

"Hear me, hear me what I say: he that strikes the first stroke, I'll run him up to the hilts, as I am a soldier"

Act II Scene I

Pist. Let floods o'erswell, and fiends for food howl on!

Nym. You'll pay me the eight shillings I won of you at betting?

Pist. Base is the slave that pays.

Nym. That now I will have; that's the humour of it,

Pist. As manhood shall compound: push home.

　　　　　　　　　　　　　　　　　　　[They draw.

Bard. By this sword, he that makes the first thrust, I'll kill him; by this sword, I will.

Pist. Sword is an oath, and oaths must have their course.

Bard. Corporal Nym, an thou wilt be friends, be friends: an thou wilt not, why then, be enemies with me too. Prithee, put up.

Nym. I shall have my eight shillings I won of you at betting?

Pist. A noble shalt thou have, and present pay;
And liquor likewise will I give to thee,
And friendship shall combine, and brotherhood:
I'll live by Nym, and Nym shall live by me.
Is not this just? for I shall sutler be
Unto the camp, and profits will accrue.
Give me thy hand.

Nym. I shall have my noble?

Pist. In cash most justly paid.

Nym. Well then, that's the humour of't.

　　　　　　　　　　Re-enter Hostess.

Host. As ever you came of women, come in quickly to Sir John. Ah, poor heart! he is so shaked of a burning quotidian tertian, that it is most lamentable to behold. Sweet men, come to him.

Nym. The king hath run bad humours on the knight; that's the even of it.

Pist.   Nym, thou hast spoke the right;
       His heart is fracted and corroborate.

Nym.   The king is a good king: but it must be as it may;
       he passes some humours and careers.

Pist.   Let us condole the knight; for, lambkins, we will live.

                         [*Exeunt.*

SCENE II.—*Southampton. A council-chamber.*

Enter EXETER, BEDFORD, *and* WESTMORELAND.

Bed.   'Fore God, his grace is bold to trust these traitors.

Exe.   They shall be apprehended by and by.

West.   How smooth and even they do bear themselves!
       As if allegiance in their bosoms sat,
       Crowned with faith and constant loyalty.

Bed.   The king hath note of all that they intend,
       By interception which they dream not of.

Exe.   Nay, but the man that was his bedfellow,
       Whom he hath dull'd and cloy'd with gracious favours,
       That he should, for a foreign purse, so sell
       His sovereign's life to death and treachery!

Trumpets sound. Enter KING HENRY, SCROOP,
       CAMBRIDGE, GREY, *and Attendants.*

K. Hen.   Now sits the wind fair, and we will aboard.
       My Lord of Cambridge, and my kind Lord of Masham,
       And you, my gentle knight, give me your thoughts:
       Think you not that the powers we bear with us
       Will cut their passage through the force of France,
       Doing the execution and the act
       For which we have in head assembled them?

Scroop.   No doubt, my liege, if each man do his best.

K. Hen.   I doubt not that; since we are well persuaded
We carry not a heart with us from hence
That grows not in a fair consent with ours;
Nor leave not one behind that doth not wish
Success and conquest to attend on us.

Cam.   Never was monarch better fear'd and lov'd
Than is your majesty: there's not, I think, a subject
That sits in heart-grief and uneasiness
Under the sweet shade of your government.

Grey.   True: those that were your father's enemies
Have steep'd their galls in honey, and do serve you
With hearts create of duty and of zeal.

K. Hen.   We therefore have great cause of thankfulness,
And shall forget the office of our hand,
Sooner than quittance of desert and merit
According to the weight and worthiness.

Scroop.   So service shall with steeled sinews toil,
And labour shall refresh itself with hope,
To do your grace incessant services.

K. Hen.   We judge no less. Uncle of Exeter,
Enlarge the man committed yesterday
That rail'd against our person: we consider
It was excess of wine that set him on;
And on his more advice we pardon him.

Scroop.   That's mercy, but too much security:
Let him be punish'd, sovereign, lest example
Breed, by his sufferance, more of such a kind.

K. Hen.   O! let us yet be merciful.

Cam.   So may your highness, and yet punish too.

Grey.   Sir,
You show great mercy, if you give him life,

After the taste of much correction.

K. Hen.   Alas! your too much love and care of me
Are heavy orisons 'gainst this poor wretch.
If little faults, proceeding on distemper,
Shall not be wink'd at, how shall we stretch our eye
When capital crimes, chew'd, swallow'd, and digested,
Appear before us? We'll yet enlarge that man,
Though Cambridge, Scroop, and Grey, in their dear care
And tender preservation of our person,
Would have him punish'd. And now to our French
    causes:
Who are the late commissioners?

Cam.   I one, my lord:
Your highness bade me ask for it to-day.

Scroop.   So did you me, my liege.

Grey.   And I, my royal sovereign.

K. Hen.   Then, Richard Earl of Cambridge, there is yours;
There yours, Lord Scroop of Masham; and, sir knight,
Grey of Northumberland, this same is yours:
Read them; and know, I know your worthiness.
My Lord of Westmoreland, and uncle Exeter,
We will aboard to-night. Why, how now, gentlemen!
What see you in those papers that you lose
So much complexion? Look ye, how they change!
Their cheeks are paper. Why, what read you there,
That hath so cowarded and chas'd your blood
Out of appearance?

Cam.   I do confess my fault,
And do submit me to your highness' mercy.

Grey, Scroop.   To which we all appeal.

K. Hen.   The mercy that was quick in us but late

By your own counsel is suppress'd and kill'd:
You must not dare, for shame, to talk of mercy;
For your own reasons turn into your bosoms,
As dogs upon their masters, worrying you.
See you, my princes and my noble peers,
These English monsters! My Lord of Cambridge here,
You know how apt our love was to accord
To furnish him with all appertinents
Belonging to his honour; and this man
Hath, for a few light crowns, lightly conspir'd,
And sworn unto the practices of France,
To kill us here in Hampton: to the which
This knight, no less for bounty bound to us
Than Cambridge is, hath likewise sworn. But O!
What shall I say to thee, Lord Scroop? thou cruel,
Ingrateful, savage and inhuman creature!
Thou that didst bear the key of all my counsels,
That knew'st the very bottom of my soul,
That almost might'st have coin'd me into gold
Would'st thou have practis'd on me for thy use,
May it be possible that foreign hire
Could out of thee extract one spark of evil
That might annoy my finger? 'tis so strange
That, though the truth of it stands off as gross
As black and white, my eye will scarcely see it.
Treason and murder ever kept together,
As two yoke-devils sworn to either's purpose,
Working so grossly in a natural cause
That admiration did not hoop at them:
But thou, 'gainst all proportion, didst bring in
Wonder to wait on treason and on murder:

And whatsoever cunning fiend it was
That wrought upon thee so preposterously
Hath got the voice in hell for excellence:
All other devils that suggest by treasons
Do botch and bungle up damnation
With patches, colours, and with forms, being fetch'd
From glistering semblances of piety;
But he that temper'd thee bade thee stand up,
Gave thee no instance why thou should'st do treason,
Unless to dub thee with the name of traitor.
If that same demon that hath gull'd thee thus
Should with his lion gait walk the whole world,
He might return to vasty Tartar back,
And tell the legions: "I can never win
A soul so easy as that Englishman's."
O! how hast thou with jealousy infected
The sweetness of affiance. Show men dutiful?
Why, so didst thou: seem they grave and learned?
Why, so didst thou: come they of noble family?
Why, so didst thou: seem they religious?
Why, so didst thou: or are they spare in diet,
Free from gross passion or of mirth or anger,
Constant in spirit, not swerving with the blood,
Garnish'd and deck'd in modest complement,
Not working with the eye without the ear,
And but in purged judgment trusting neither?
Such and so finely bolted didst thou seem:
And thus thy fall hath left a kind of blot,
To mark the full-fraught man and best indued
With some suspicion. I will weep for thee;
For this revolt of thine, methinks, is like

"Cheerly to sea; the signs of war advance:
No king of England, if not king of France"

Another fall of man. Their faults are open:
Arrest them to the answer of the law;
And God acquit them of their practices!

Exe. I arrest thee of high treason, by the name of
Richard Earl of Cambridge.
I arrest thee of high treason, by the name of
Henry Lord Scroop of Masham.
I arrest thee of high treason, by the name of
Thomas Grey, knight, of Northumberland.

Scroop. Our purposes God justly hath discover'd,
And I repent my fault more than my death;
Which I beseech your highness to forgive,
Although my body pay the price of it.

Cam. For me, the gold of France did not seduce,
Although I did admit it as a motive
The sooner to effect what I intended:
But God be thanked for prevention;
Which I in sufferance heartily will rejoice,
Beseeching God and you to pardon me.

Grey. Never did faithful subject more rejoice
At the discovery of most dangerous treason
Than I do at this hour joy o'er myself,
Prevented from a damned enterprise.
My fault, but not my body, pardon, sovereign.

K. Hen. God quit you in his mercy! Hear your sentence.
You have conspir'd against our royal person,
Join'd with an enemy proclaim'd, and from his coffers
Receiv'd the golden earnest of our death;
Wherein you would have sold your king to slaughter,
His princes and his peers to servitude,
His subjects to oppression and contempt,

And his whole kingdom into desolation.
Touching our person seek we no revenge;
But we our kingdom's safety must so tender,
Whose ruin you have sought, that to her laws
We do deliver you. Get you therefore hence,
Poor miserable wretches, to your death;
The taste whereof, God of his mercy give you
Patience to endure, and true repentance
Of all your dear offences! Bear them hence.

        [Exeunt Cambridge, Scroop, and Grey, guarded.
Now, lords, for France; the enterprise whereof
Shall be to you, as us, like glorious.
We doubt not of a fair and lucky war,
Since God so graciously hath brought to light
This dangerous treason lurking in our way
To hinder our beginnings. We doubt not now
But every rub is smoothed on our way.
Then forth, dear countrymen: let us deliver
Our puissance into the hand of God,
Putting it straight in expedition.
Cheerly to sea; the signs of war advance:
No king of England, if not king of France.   *[Exeunt.*

SCENE III.—*London. Before a Tavern.*

Enter PISTOL, *Hostess,* NYM, BARDOLPH, *and Boy.*

Host.   Prithee, honey-sweet husband, let me bring thee
    to Staines.
Pist.   No; for my manly heart doth earn.
    Bardolph, be blithe; Nym, rouse thy vaunting veins:
    Boy, bristle thy courage up; for Falstaff he is dead,
    And we must earn therefore.

Bard.   Would I were with him, wheresome'er he is, either in heaven or in hell!

Host.   Nay, sure, he's not in hell: he's in Arthur's bosom, if ever man went to Arthur's bosom. A' made a finer end —and went away an it had been any christom child; a' parted even just between twelve and one, even at the turning o' the tide: for after I saw him fumble with the sheets and play with flowers and smile upon his fingers' ends, I knew there was but one way; for his nose was as sharp as a pen, and a' babled of green fields. "How now, Sir John?" quoth I: "what, man! be o' good cheer." So a' cried out "God, God, God!" three or four times: now I, to comfort him, bid him a' should not think of God, I hoped there was no need to trouble himself with any such thoughts yet. So a' bade me lay more clothes on his feet: I put my hand into the bed and felt them, and they were as cold as any stone; then I felt to his knees, and so upward, and upward, and all was as cold as any stone.

Nym.   They say he cried out of sack.

Host.   Ay, that a' did.

Bard.   And of women.

Host.   Nay, that a' did not.

Boy.   Yes, that a' did; and said they were devils incarnate.

Host.   A' could never abide carnation; 'twas a colour he never liked.

Boy.   A' said once, the devil would have him about women.

Host.   A' did in some sort, indeed, handle women; but then he was rheumatic, and talked of the whore of Babylon.

Boy.   Do you not remember a' saw a flea stick upon Bardolph's nose, and a' said it was a black soul burning in hell-fire?

Bard.   Well, the fuel is gone that maintained that fire:
     that's all the riches I got in his service.
Nym.   Shall we shog? the king will be gone from
     Southampton.
Pist.   Come, let's away. My love, give me thy lips.
     Look to my chattels and my moveables:
     Let senses rule, the word is "Pitch and pay";
     Trust none;
     For oaths are straws, men's faiths are wafer-cakes,
     And hold-fast is the only dog, my duck:
     Therefore, Caveto be thy counsellor.
     Go, clear thy crystals. Yoke-fellows in arms,
     Let us to France; like horse-leeches, my boys,
     To suck, to suck, the very blood to suck!
Boy.   And that's but unwholesome food, they say.
Pist.   Touch her soft mouth, and march.
Bard.   Farewell, hostess.   *[Kissing her.*
Nym.   I cannot kiss, that is the humour of it; but adieu.
Pist.   Let housewifery appear: keep close, I thee command.
Host.   Farewell; adieu.   *[Exeunt.*

SCENE IV.—*France. The French King's Palace.*

Flourish. Enter the French KING, *attended; the* DAUPHIN, *the Dukes of* BERRI *and* BRETAGNE, *the Constable, and others.*

Fr. King.   Thus comes the English with full power upon us;
     And more than carefully it us concerns
     To answer royally in our defences.
     Therefore the Dukes of Berri and of Bretagne,
     Of Brabant and of Orleans, shall make forth,
     And you, Prince Dauphin, with all swift dispatch,

"*And more than carefully it us concerns*
To answer royally in our defences"

To line and new repair our towns of war
With men of courage and with means defendant;
For England his approaches makes as fierce
As waters to the sucking of a gulf.
It fits us then to be as provident
As fear may teach us out of late examples
Left by the fatal and neglected English
Upon our fields.

Dau.   My most redoubted father,
It is most meet we arm us 'gainst the foe;
For peace itself should not so dull a kingdom,
Though war nor no known quarrel were in question,
But that defences, musters, preparations,
Should be maintain'd, assembled, and collected,
As were a war in expectation.
Therefore, I say 'tis meet we all go forth
To view the sick and feeble parts of France:
And let us do it with no show of fear;
No, with no more than if we heard that England
Were busied with a Whitsun morris-dance:
For, my good liege, she is so idly king'd
Her sceptre so fantastically borne
By a vain, giddy, shallow, humorous youth,
That fear attends her not.

Con.   O peace, Prince Dauphin!
You are too much mistaken in this king.
Question your grace the late ambassadors,
With what great state he heard their embassy,
How well supplied with noble counsellors.
How modest in exception, and withal
How terrible in constant resolution,

And you shall find his vanities forespent
Were but the outside of the Roman Brutus,
Covering discretion with a coat of folly;
As gardeners do with ordure hide those roots
That shall first spring and be most delicate.

Dau.   Well, 'tis not so, my lord high constable;
But though we think it so, it is no matter:
In cases of defence 'tis best to weigh
The enemy more mighty than he seems:
So the proportions of defence are fill'd;
Which of a weak and niggardly projection
Doth, like a miser, spoil his coat with scanting
A little cloth.

Fr. King.   Think we King Harry strong;
And, princes, look you strongly arm to meet him.
The kindred of him hath been flesh'd upon us,
And he is bred out of that bloody strain
That haunted us in our familiar paths:
Witness our too much memorable shame
When Cressy battle fatally was struck,
And all our princes captiv'd by the hand
Of that black name, Edward, Black Prince of Wales;
Whiles that his mountain sire, on mountain standing,
Up in the air, crown'd with the golden sun,
Saw his heroical seed, and smil'd to see him,
Mangle the work of nature, and deface
The patterns that by God and by French fathers
Had twenty years been made. This is a stem
Of that victorious stock; and let us fear
The native mightiness and fate of him.

Enter a Messenger.

Mess. Ambassadors from Harry King of England
Do crave admittance to your majesty.
Fr. King. We'll give them present audience. Go, and bring
them.

                    [Exeunt Messenger and certain Lords.
You see this chase is hotly follow'd, friends.
Dau. Turn head, and stop pursuit; for coward dogs
Most spend their mouths when what they seem to
      threaten
Runs far before them. Good my sovereign,
Take up the English short, and let them know
Of what a monarchy you are the head:
Self-love, my liege, is not so vile a sin
As self-neglecting.

        Re-enter Lords, with EXETER *and Train.*

Fr. King. From our brother of England?
Exe. From him; and thus he greets your majesty.
He wills you, in the name of God Almighty,
That you divest yourself, and lay apart
The borrow'd glories that by gift of heaven,
By law of nature and of nations, longs
To him and to his heirs; namely, the crown
And all wide-stretched honours that pertain
By custom and the ordinance of times
Unto the crown of France. That you may know
'Tis no sinister nor no awkward claim,
Pick'd from the worm-holes of long-vanish'd days,
Nor from the dust of old oblivion rak'd,
He sends you this most memorable line,

In every branch truly demonstrative;
Willing you overlook this pedigree;
And when you find him evenly deriv'd
From his most fam'd of famous ancestors,
Edward the Third, he bids you then resign
Your crown and kingdom, indirectly held
From him the native and true challenger.

Fr. King.   Or else what follows?

Exe.   Bloody constraint; for if you hide the crown
Even in your hearts, there will he rake for it:
Therefore in fierce tempest is he coming,
In thunder and in earthquake like a Jove,
That, if requiring fail, he will compel;
And bids you, in the bowels of the Lord,
Deliver up the crown, and to take mercy
On the poor souls for whom this hungry war
Opens his vasty jaws; and on your head
Turning the widows' tears, the orphans' cries,
The dead men's blood, the pining maidens' groans,
For husbands, fathers, and betrothed lovers,
That shall be swallow'd in this controversy.
This is his claim, his threat'ning, and my message;
Unless the Dauphin be in presence here,
To whom expressly I bring greeting too.

Fr. King.   For us, we will consider of this further:
To-morrow shall you bear our full intent
Back to our brother of England.

Dau.   For the Dauphin,
I stand here for him: what to him from England?

Exe.   Scorn and defiance; slight regard, contempt,
And any thing that may not misbecome

The mighty sender, doth he prize you at.
Thus says my king: an if your father's highness
Do not, in grant of all demands at large,
Sweeten the bitter mock you sent his majesty,
He'll call you to so hot an answer of it,
That caves and womby vaultages of France
Shall chide your trespass and return your mock
In second accent of his ordinance.

Dau. Say, if my father render fair return,
It is against my will; for I desire
Nothing but odds with England: to that end,
As matching to his youth and vanity,
I did present him with the Paris balls.

Exe. He'll make your Paris Louvre shake for it,
Were it the mistress-court of mighty Europe:
And, be assur'd, you'll find a difference,
As we his subjects have in wonder found,
Between the promise of his greener days
And these he masters now. Now he weighs time
Even to the utmost grain; that you shall read
In your own losses, if he stay in France.

Fr. King. To-morrow shall you know our mind at full.

Exe. Dispatch us with all speed, lest that our king
Come here himself to question our delay;
For he is footed in this land already.

Fr. King. You shall be soon dispatch'd with fair conditions:
A night is but small breath and little pause
To answer matters of this consequence.

[Flourish. Exeunt.

ACT III

Enter CHORUS.

Thus with imagin'd wing our swift scene flies
In motion of no less celerity
Than that of thought. Suppose that you have seen
The well-appointed king at Hampton pier
Embark his royalty; and his brave fleet
With silken streamers the young Phœbus fanning:
Play with your fancies, and in them behold
Upon the hempen tackle ship-boys climbing;
Hear the shrill whistle which doth order give
To sounds confus'd; behold the threaden sails,
Borne with the invisible and creeping wind,
Draw the huge bottoms through the furrow'd sea,
Breasting the lofty surge. O! do but think
You stand upon the rivage and behold
A city on the inconstant billows dancing;
For so appears this fleet majestical,
Holding due course to Harfleur. Follow, follow!
Grapple your minds to sternage of this navy,
And leave your England, as dead midnight still,
Guarded with grandsires, babies, and old women,
Either past or not arriv'd to pith and puissance:
For who is he, whose chin is but enrich'd
With one appearing hair, that will not follow
These cull'd and choice-drawn cavaliers to France?
Work, work your thoughts, and therein see a siege;
Behold the ordinance on their carriages,
With fatal mouths gaping on girded Harfleur.
Suppose the ambassador from the French comes back;

"Thus with imagin'd wing our swift scene flies
In motion of no less celerity than that of thought"

Tells Harry that the king doth offer him
Katharine his daughter; and with her, to dowry,
Some petty and unprofitable dukedoms:
The offer likes not: and the nimble gunner
With linstock now the devilish cannon touches,

                  [Alarum, and chambers go off.

And down goes all before them. Still be kind,
And eche out our performance with your mind.   *[Exit.*

        SCENE I.—*France. Before Harfleur.*

Alarums. Enter KING HENRY, EXETER, BEDFORD,
    GLOUCESTER, *and Soldiers, with scaling-ladders.*

K. Hen. Once more unto the breach, dear friends, once more,
  Or close the wall up with our English dead.
  In peace there's nothing so becomes a man
  As modest stillness and humility:
  But when the blast of war blows in our ears,
  Then imitate the action of the tiger;
  Stiffen the sinews, summon up the blood,
  Disguise fair nature with hard-favour'd rage;
  Then lend the eye a terrible aspect;
  Let it pry through the portage of the head
  Like the brass cannon; let the brow o'erwhelm it
  As fearfully as doth a galled rock
  O'erhang and jutty his confounded base,
  Swill'd with the wild and wasteful ocean.
  Now set the teeth and stretch the nostril wide,
  Hold hard the breath, and bend up every spirit
  To his full height! On, on, you noblest English!
  Whose blood is fet from fathers of war-proof;

Fathers that, like so many Alexanders,
Have in these parts from morn till even fought,
And sheath'd their swords for lack of argument.
Dishonour not your mothers; now attest
That those whom you call'd fathers did beget you.
Be copy now to men of grosser blood,
And teach them how to war. And you, good yeomen,
Whose limbs were made in England, show us here
The mettle of your pasture; let us swear
That you are worth your breeding; which I doubt not;
For there is none of you so mean and base
That hath not noble lustre in your eyes.
I see you stand like greyhounds in the slips,
Straining upon the start. The game's afoot:
Follow your spirit; and upon this charge
Cry, "God for Harry, England, and Saint George!"

[*Exeunt. Alarum, and chambers go off.*

SCENE II.—*The Same.*

Enter NYM, BARDOLPH, PISTOL, *and Boy.*

Bard.   On, on, on, on, on! to the breach, to the breach!

Nym.   Pray thee, corporal, stay: the knocks are too hot;
and for mine own part, I have not a case of lives:
the humour of it is too hot, that is the very plain-song
of it.

Pist.   The plain-song is most just, for humours do abound:

> *Knocks go and come, God's vassals drop and die;*
> *And sword and shield,*
> *In bloody field,*
> *Doth win immortal fame.*

Boy. Would I were in an alehouse in London! I would
give all my fame for a pot of ale, and safety.

Pist. And I: *If wishes would prevail with me,*
My purpose should not fail with me,
But thither would I hie.

Boy. *As duly, but not as truly,*
As bird doth sing on bough.

Enter FLUELLEN.

Flu. Up to the breach, you dogs! avaunt, you cullions!
[Driving them forward.

Pist. Be merciful, great duke, to men of mould!
Abate thy rage, abate thy manly rage;
Abate thy rage, great duke!
Good bawcock, bate thy rage; use lenity, sweet chuck!

Nym. These be good humours! your honour wins bad
humours. *[Exeunt all but Boy.*

Boy. As young as I am, I have observed these three swash-
ers. I am boy to them all three, but all they three, though
they would serve me, could not be man to me; for indeed
three such antics do not amount to a man. For Bardolph,
he is white-livered and red-faced; by the means whereof
a' faces it out, but fights not. For Pistol, he hath a killing
tongue and a quiet sword; by the means whereof a' breaks
words, and keeps whole weapons. For Nym, he hath
heard that men of few words are the best men; and therefore he scorns to say his prayers, lest a' should be thought
a coward: but his few bad words are matched with as
few good deeds; for a' never broke any man's head but
his own, and that was against a post when he was drunk.
They will steal any thing and call it purchase. Bardolph

stole a lute-case, bore it twelve leagues, and sold it for three half-pence. Nym and Bardolph are sworn brothers in filching, and in Calais they stole a fire-shovel; I knew by that piece of service the men would carry coals. They would have me as familiar with men's pockets as their gloves or their handkerchers: which makes much against my manhood if I should take from another's pocket to put into mine; for it is plain pocketing up of wrongs. I must leave them and seek some better service: their villany goes against my weak stomach, and therefore I must cast it up.   [*Exit*.

Re-enter FLUELLEN, GOWER *following*.

Gow.   Captain Fluellen, you must come presently to the mines; the Duke of Gloucester would speak with you.

Flu.   To the mines! tell you the duke it is not so good to come to the mines. For look you, the mines is not according to the disciplines of the war; the concavities of it is not sufficient; for, look you, th' athversary, you may discuss unto the duke, look you, is digt himself four yard under with countermines. By Cheshu, I think a' will plough up all if there is not better directions.

Gow.   The Duke of Gloucester, to whom the order of the siege is given, is altogether directed by an Irishman, a very valiant gentleman, i' faith.

Flu.   It is Captain Macmorris, is it not?

Gow.   I think it be.

Flu.   By Cheshu, he is an ass, as in the world: I will verify as much in his beard: he has no more directions in the true disciplines of the wars, look you, of the Roman disciplines, than is a puppy-dog.

"Captain Macmorris, I beseech you now, will you vout-
safe me, look you, a few disputations with you"

Enter MACMORRIS *and* JAMY, *at a distance.*

Gow.   Here a' comes; and the Scots captain, Captain Jamy, with him.

Flu.   Captain Jamy is a marvellous falorous gentleman, that is certain; and of great expedition and knowledge in th' aunchient wars, upon my particular knowledge of his directions: by Cheshu, he will maintain his argument as well as any military man in the world, in the disciplines of the pristine wars of the Romans.

Jamy.   I say gud day, Captain Fluellen.

Flu.   God-den to your worship, good Captain James.

Gow.   How now, Captain Macmorris! have you quit the mines? have the pioners given o'er?

Mac.   By Chrish, la! tish ill done: the work ish give over, the trompet sound the retreat. By my hand, I swear, and my father's soul, the work ish ill done; it ish give over: I would have blowed up the town, so Chrish save me, la! in an hour: O! tish ill done, tish ill done; by my hand, tish ill done.

Flu.   Captain Macmorris, I beseech you now, will you voutsafe me, look you, a few disputations with you, as partly touching or concerning the disciplines of the war, the Roman wars, in the way of argument, look you, and friendly communication; partly to satisfy my opinion, and partly for the satisfaction, look you, of my mind, as touching the direction of the military discipline: that is the point.

Jamy.   It sall be vary gud, gud feith, gud captains bath: and I sall quit you with gud leve, as I may pick occasion; that sall I, marry.

Mac.   It is no time to discourse, so Chrish save me: the day is hot, and the weather, and the wars, and the king, and the dukes: it is no time to discourse. The town is beseeched, and the trumpet call us to the breach; and we talk, and, be Chrish, do nothing: 'tis shame for us all; so God sa'me, 'tis shame to stand still; it is shame, by my hand; and there is throats to be cut, and works to be done; and there ish nothing done, so Chrish sa' me, la!

Jamy.   By the mess, ere theise eyes of mine take themselves to slomber, aile de gud service, or aile lig i' the grund for it; ay, or go to death; and aile pay it as valorously as I may, that sall I suerly do, that is the breff and the long. Marry, I wad full fain heard some question 'tween you tway.

Flu.   Captain Macmorris, I think, look you, under your correction, there is not many of your nation—

Mac.   Of my nation! What ish my nation? Ish a villain, and a bastard, and a knave, and a rascal— What ish my nation? Who talks of my nation?

Flu.   Look you, if you take the matter otherwise than is meant, Captain Macmorris, peradventure I shall think you do not use me with that affability as in discretion you ought to use me, look you; being as good as man as yourself, both in the disciplines of war, and in the derivation of my birth, and in other particularities.

Mac.   I do not know you so good a man as myself: so Chrish save me, I will cut off your head.

Gow.   Gentlemen both, you will mistake each other.

Jamy.   A! that's a foul fault.   [*A parley sounded.*

Gow.   The town sounds a parley.

Flu.   Captain Macmorris, when there is more better opportunity to be required, look you, I will be so bold as to

tell you I know the disciplines of war; and there is an
end.   [*Exeunt.*

SCENE III.—*The Same. Before the Gates.*

*The Governor and some Citizens on the walls ; the English Forces
below. Enter* KING HENRY *and his Train.*

K. *Hen.*   How yet resolves the governor of the town?
This is the latest parle we will admit:
Therefore to our best mercy give yourselves;
Or like to men proud of destruction
Defy us to our worst: for, as I am a soldier,
A name that in my thoughts becomes me best,
If I begin the battery once again,
I will not leave the half-achieved Harfleur
Till in her ashes she lied buried.
The gates of mercy shall be all shut up,
And the flesh'd soldier, rough and hard of heart,
In liberty of bloody hand shall range
With conscience wide as hell, mowing like grass
Your fresh-air virgins and your flowering infants.
What is it then to me, if impious war,
Array'd in flames like to the prince of fiends,
Do, with his smirch'd complexion, all fell feats
Enlink'd to waste and desolation?
What is't to me, when you yourselves are cause,
If your pure maidens fall into the hand
Of hot and forcing violation?
What rein can hold licentious wickedness
When down the hill he holds his fierce career?
We may as bootless spend our vain command

Upon the enraged soldiers in their spoil
As send precepts to the leviathan
To come ashore. Therefore, you men of Harfleur,
Take pity of your town and of your people,
Whiles yet my soldiers are in my command;
Whiles yet the cool and temperate wind of grace
O'erblows the filthy and contagious clouds
Of heady murder, spoil, and villany.
If not, why, in a moment look to see
The blind and bloody soldier with foul hand
Defile the locks of your shrill-shrieking daughters;
Your fathers taken by the silver beards,
And their most reverend heads dash'd to the walls;
Your naked infants spitted upon pikes,
Whiles the mad mothers with their howls confus'd
Do break the clouds, as did the wives of Jewry
At Herod's bloody-hunting slaughtermen.
What say you? will you yield, and this avoid?
Or, guilty in defence, be thus destroy'd?

Gov.   Our expectation hath this day an end.
The Dauphin, whom of succours we entreated,
Returns us that his powers are yet not ready
To raise so great a siege. Therefore, great king,
We yield our town and lives to thy soft mercy.
Enter our gates; dispose of us and ours;
For we no longer are defensible.

K. Hen.   Open your gates! Come, uncle Exeter,
Go you and enter Harfleur; there remain,
And fortify it strongly 'gainst the French:
Use mercy to them all. For us, dear uncle,
The winter coming on and sickness growing

Upon our soldiers, we will retire to Calais.
To-night in Harfleur will we be your guest;
To-morrow for the march are we addrest.

> [*Flourish. The King and his train enter the town.*

SCENE IV.—*Rouen. A Room in the Palace.*

Enter KATHARINE *and* ALICE.

Kath. Alice, tu as esté en Angleterre, et tu parles bien le langage.

Alice. Un peu, madame.

Kath. Je te prie, m' enseignez; il faut que j' apprenne à parler. Comment appellez vous la main en Anglois?

Alice. La main? elle est appellée de hand.

Kath. De hand. Et les doigts?

Alice. Les doigts? ma foy, je oublie les doigts, mais je me souviendray. Les doigts? je pense qu'ils sont appellés de fingres; ouy, de fingres.

Kath. La main, de hand; les doigts, de fingres. Je pense que je suis le bon escolier. J'ai gagné deux mots d'Anglois vistement. Comment appellez vous les ongles?

Alice. Les ongles? nous les appellons de nails.

Kath. De nails. Escoutez; dites moy si je parle bien: de hand, de fingres, et de nails.

Alice. C'est bien dict, madame; il est fort bon Anglois.

Kath. Dites moy l'Anglois pour le bras.

Alice. De arm, madame.

Kath. Et le coude?

Alice. De elbow.

Kath. De elbow. Je m'en fais la répétition de tous les mots que vous m' avez appris dès à présent.

Alice. Il est trop difficile, madame, comme je pense.

Kath.   *Excusez moy, Alice; escoutez: de hand, de fingres, de nails, de arma, de bilbow.*

Alice.   *De elbow, madame.*

Kath.   *O Seigneur Dieu! je m'en oublie; de elbow. Comment appellez vous le col?*

Alice.   *De nick, madame.*

Kath.   *De nick. Et le menton?*

Alice.   *De chin.*

Kath.   *De sin. Le col, de nick; le menton, de sin.*

Alice.   *Ouy. Sauf vostre honneur, en vérité, vous prononcez les mots aussi droict que les natifs d'Angleterre.*

Kath.   *Je ne doute point d'apprendre par la grace de Dieu, et en peu de temps.*

Alice.   *N'avez vous déja oublié ce que je vous ay enseigné?*

Kath.   *Non, je reciteray à vous promptement. De hand, de fingre, de mails—*

Alice.   *De nails, madame.*

Kath.   *De nails, de arme, de ilbow.*

Alice.   *Sauf vostre honneur, d'elbow.*

Kath.   *Ainsi dis je; d'elbow, de nick, et de sin. Comment appellez vous le pied et la robe?*

Alice.   *Le foot, madame; et le coun.*

Kath.   *Le foot, et le coun? O Seigneur Dieu! ils sont les mots de son mauvais, corruptible, gros, et impudique, et non pour les dames d'honneur d'user. Je ne voudrois prononcer ces mots devant les seigneurs de France, pour tout le monde. Foh! le foot et le coun! Néant-moins je reciteray une autre fois ma leçon ensemble: d'hand, de fingre, de nails, d'arm, d'elbow, de nick, de sin, de foot, le coun.*

Alice.   *Excellent, madame!*

Kath.   *C'est assez pour une fois: allons nous à diner.* [*Exeunt.*

"La main? elle est appellée hand"

SCENE V.—*The Same.*

Enter the King of France, the DAUPHIN, *the Duke of* BOURBON, *the Constable of France, and others.*

Fr. King. 'Tis certain he hath pass'd the river Somme.
Con. And if he be not fought withal, my lord,
  Let us not live in France; let us quit all,
  And give our vineyards to a barbarous people.
Dau. O *Dieu vivant!* shall a few sprays of us,
  The emptying of our fathers' luxury,
  Our scions, put in wild and savage stock,
  Spirt up so suddenly into the clouds,
  And overlook their grafters?
Bour. Normans, but bastard Normans, Norman bastards!
  Mort de ma vie! if they march along
  Unfought withal, but I will sell my dukedom,
  To buy a slobbery and a dirty farm
  In that nook-shotten isle of Albion.
Con. *Dieu de batailles!* where have they this mettle?
  Is not their climate foggy, raw and dull,
  On whom, as in despite, the sun looks pale,
  Killing their fruit with frowns? Can sodden water,
  A drench for sur-rein'd jades, their barley broth,
  Decoct their cold blood to such valiant heat?
  And shall our quick blood, spirited with wine,
  Seem frosty? O, for honour of our land,
  Let us not hang like roping icicles
  Upon our houses' thatch, whiles a more frosty people
  Sweat drops of gallant youth in our rich fields!—
  Poor we may call them in their native lords.
Dau. By faith and honour,

　　　　Our madams mock at us, and plainly say
　　　　Our mettle is bred out; and they will give
　　　　Their bodies to the lust of English youth
　　　　To new-store France with bastard warriors.
Bour.　　They bid us to the English dancing-schools,
　　　　And teach lavoltas high and swift corantos;
　　　　Saying our grace is only in our heels,
　　　　And that we are most lofty runaways.
Fr. King.　　Where is Montjoy the herald? speed him hence:
　　　　Let him greet England with our sharp defiance.
　　　　Up, princes! and, with spirit of honour edg'd
　　　　More sharper than your swords, hie to the field:
　　　　Charles Delabreth, high constable of France;
　　　　You Dukes of Orleans, Bourbon, and of Berri,
　　　　Alençon, Brabant, Bar, and Burgundy;
　　　　Jaques Chatillon, Rambures, Vaudemont,
　　　　Beaumont, Grandpré, Roussi, and Fauconberg,
　　　　Foix, Lestrale, Bouciqualt, and Charolois;
　　　　High dukes, great princes, barons, lords, and knights,
　　　　For your great seats now quit you of great shames,
　　　　Bar Harry England, that sweeps through our land
　　　　With pennons painted in the blood of Harfleur:
　　　　Rush on his host, as doth the melted snow
　　　　Upon the valleys, whose low vassal seat
　　　　The Alps doth spit and void his rheum upon:
　　　　Go down upon him, you have power enough,
　　　　And in a captive chariot into Roan
　　　　Bring him our prisoner.
Con.　　This becomes the great.
　　　　Sorry am I his numbers are so few,
　　　　His soldiers sick and famish'd in their march,

For I am sure when he shall see our army
He'll drop his heart into the sink of fear,
And for achievement offer us his ransom.

Fr. King.   Therefore, lord constable, haste on Montjoy,
And let him say to England that we send
To know what willing ransom he will give.
Prince Dauphin, you shall stay with us in Roan.

Dau.   Not so, I do beseech your majesty.

Fr. King.   Be patient, for you shall remain with us.
Now forth, lord constable and princes all,
And quickly bring us word of England's fall.   [*Exeunt.*

SCENE VI.—*The English Camp in Picardy.*

Enter GOWER *and* FLUELLEN.

Gow.   How now, Captain Fluellen! come you from the
bridge?

Flu.   I assure you there is very excellent services committed
at the bridge.

Gow.   Is the Duke of Exeter safe?

Flu.   The Duke of Exeter is as magnanimous as Agamem-
non; and a man that I love and honour with my soul,
and my heart, and my duty, and my life, and my living,
and my uttermost power: he is not—God be praised and
blessed!—any hurt in the world, but keeps the bridge
most valiantly, with excellent discipline. There is an aunchient lieutenant there at the pridge; I think in my very
conscience he is as valiant a man as Mark Antony; and
he is a man of no estimation in the world; but I did see
him do as gallant service.

Gow.   What do you call him?

Flu.   He is called Aunchient Pistol.

Gow.   I know him not.

Enter PISTOL.

Flu.   Here is the man.

Pist.   Captain, I thee beseech to do me favours: The Duke of Exeter doth love thee well.

Flu.   Ay, I praise God; and I have merited some love at his hands.

Pist.   Bardolph, a soldier firm and sound of heart,
And of buxom valour, hath, by cruel fate
And giddy Fortune's furious fickle wheel,
That goddess blind,
That stands upon the rolling restless stone—

Flu.   By your patience, Aunchient Pistol. Fortune is painted blind, with a muffler afore her eyes, to signify to you that Fortune is blind: and she is painted also with a wheel, to signify to you, which is the moral of it, that she is turning, and inconstant, and mutability, and variation: and her foot, look you, is fixed upon a spherical stone, which rolls, and rolls, and rolls: in good truth, the poet makes a most excellent description of it: Fortune is an excellent moral.

Pist.   Fortune is Bardolph's foe, and frowns on him;
For he hath stol'n a pax, and hanged must a' be.
A damned death!
Let gallows gape for dog, let man go free
And let not hemp his wind-pipe suffocate.
But Exeter hath given the doom of death
For pax of little price.
Therefore, go speak; the duke will hear thy voice;
And let not Bardolph's vital thread be cut

"Now forth, lord constable and princes all,
And quickly bring us word of England's fall"

With edge of penny cord and vile reproach:
Speak, captain, for his life, and I will thee requite.

Flu.   Aunchient Pistol, I do partly understand your
meaning.

Pist.   Why then, rejoice therefore.

Flu.   Certainly, aunchient, it is not a thing to rejoice at; for
if, look you, he were my brother, I would desire the duke
to use his good pleasure and put him to execution; for
discipline ought to be used.

Pist.   Die and be damn'd; and figo for thy friendship!

Flu.   It is well.

Pist.   The fig of Spain!   [*Exit.*

Flu.   Very good.

Gow.   Why, this is an arrant counterfeit rascal: I remember
him now; a bawd, a cut-purse.

Flu.   I'll assure you a' uttered as prave words at the pridge
as you shall see in a summer's day. But it is very well;
what he has spoke to me, that is well, I warrant you,
when time is serve.

Gow.   Why, 'tis a gull, a fool, a rogue, that now and then
goes to the wars to grace himself at his return into London under the form of a soldier. And such fellows are
perfect in the great commanders' names, and they will
learn you by rote where services were done; at such and
such a sconce, at such a breach, at such a convoy; who
came off bravely, who was shot, who disgraced, what
terms the enemy stood on; and this they con perfectly
in the phrase of war, which they trick up with new-tuned
oaths: and what a beard of the general's cut and a horrid
suit of the camp will do among foaming bottles and ale-
washed wits, is wonderful to be thought on. But you

must learn to know such slanders of the age, or else you may be marvellously mistook.

Flu.   I tell you what, Captain Gower; I do perceive he is not the man that he would gladly make show to the world he is: if I find a hole in his coat I will tell him my mind.   [*Drum heard.*

Hark you, the king is coming, and I must speak with him from the pridge.

Drum and Colours. Enter KING HENRY, GLOUCESTER, *and Soldiers.*

Flu.   God pless your majesty!

K. Hen.   How now, Fluellen! camest thou from the bridge?

Flu.   Ay, so please your majesty. The Duke of Exeter has very gallantly maintained the pridge: the French is gone off, look you, and there is gallant and most prave passages. Marry, th' athversary was have possession of the pridge, but he is enforced to retire, and the Duke of Exeter is master of the pridge. I can tell your majesty the duke is a prave man.

K. Hen.   What men have you lost, Fluellen?

Flu.   The perdition of th' athversary hath been very great, reasonable great: marry, for my part, I think the duke hath lost never a man but one that is like to be executed for robbing a church; one Bardolph, if your majesty know the man: his face is all bubukles, and whelks, and knobs, and flames o' fire; and his lips blows at his nose, and it is like a coal of fire, sometimes plue and sometimes red; but his nose is executed, and his fire's out.

K. Hen.   We would have all such offenders so cut off: and we give express charge that in our marches through the country there be nothing compelled from the villages, nothing taken but paid for, none of the French upbraided or abused in disdainful language; for when lenity and cruelty play for a kingdom, the gentler gamester is the soonest winner.

Tucket. Enter MONTJOY.

Mont.   You know me by my habit.

K. Hen.   Well then I know thee: what shall I know of thee?

Mont.   My master's mind.

K. Hen.   Unfold it.

Mont.   Thus says my king: Say thou to Harry of England: Though we seemed dead, we did but sleep: advantage is a better soldier than rashness. Tell him we could have rebuked him at Harfleur, but that we thought not good to bruise an injury till it were full ripe: now we speak upon our cue, and our voice is imperial: England shall repent his folly, see his weakness, and admire our sufferance. Bid him therefore consider of his ransom; which must proportion the losses we have borne, the subjects we have lost, the disgrace we have digested; which in weight to re-answer, his pettiness would bow under. For our losses, his exchequer is too poor; for the effusion of our blood, the muster of his kingdom too faint a number; and for our disgrace, his own person, kneeling at our feet, but a weak and worthless satisfaction. To this add defiance: and tell him, for conclusion, he hath betrayed his followers, whose condemnation is pronounced. So far my king and master, so much my office.

K. Hen.   What is thy name? I know thy quality.

Mont.   Montjoy.

K. Hen.   Thou dost thy office fairly. Turn thee back,
And tell thy king I do not seek him now,
But could be willing to march on to Calais
Without impeachment; for, to say the sooth,
Though 'tis no wisdom to confess so much
Unto an enemy of craft and vantage,
My people are with sickness much enfeebled,
My numbers lessen'd, and those few I have
Almost no better than so many French;
Who when they were in health, I tell thee, herald,
I thought upon one pair of English legs
Did march three Frenchmen. Yet, forgive me, God,
That I do brag thus! this your air of France
Hath blown that vice in me; I must repent.
Go therefore, tell thy master here I am;
My ransom is this frail and worthless trunk,
My army but a weak and sickly guard;
Yet, God before, tell him we will come on,
Though France himself and such another neighbour
Stand in our way. There's for thy labour, Montjoy.
Go, bid thy master well advise himself:
If we may pass, we will; if we be hinder'd,
We shall your tawny ground with your red blood
Discolour: and so, Montjoy, fare you well.
The sum of all our answer is but this:
We would not seek a battle as we are;
Nor, as we are, we say we will not shun it:
So tell your master.

Mont.   I shall deliver so. Thanks to your highness.   [*Exit.*

Glou.   I hope they will not come upon us now.

K. Hen.   We are in God's hand, brother, not in theirs.

March to the bridge; it now draws toward night:
Beyond the river we'll encamp ourselves,
And on to-morrow bid them march away.   [*Exeunt.*

SCENE VII.—*The French Camp, near Agincourt.*

Enter the Constable of France, the LORD RAMBURES,
ORLEANS, DAUPHIN, *with others.*

Con.   Tut! I have the best armour of the world. Would it
were day!

Orl.   You have an excellent armour; but let my horse have
his due.

Con.   It is the best horse of Europe.

Orl.   Will it never be morning?

Dau.   My lord of Orleans, and my lord high constable, you
talk of horse and armour?

Orl.   You are as well provided of both as any prince in the
world.

Dau.   What a long night is this! I will not change my horse
with any that treads but on four pasterns. *Ça,* ha! He
bounds from the earth as if his entrails were hairs; *le
cheval volant,* the Pegasus, *chez les narines de feu!* When
I bestride him, I soar, I am a hawk: he trots the air; the
earth sings when he touches it; the basest horn of his
hoof is more musical than the pipe of Hermes.

Orl.   He's of the colour of the nutmeg.

Dau.   And of the heat of the ginger. It is a beast for Perseus:
he is pure air and fire; and the dull elements of earth
and water never appear in him, but only in patient stillness while his rider mounts him: he is indeed a horse:
and all other jades you may call beasts.

Con.   Indeed, my lord, it is a most absolute and excellent horse.

Dau.   It is the prince of palfreys; his neigh is like the bidding of a monarch, and his countenance enforces homage.

Orl.   No more, cousin.

Dau.   Nay, the man hath no wit that cannot, from the rising of the lark to the lodging of the lamb, vary deserved praise on my palfrey: it is a theme as fluent as the sea; turn the sands into eloquent tongues, and my horse is argument for them all. 'Tis a subject for a sovereign to reason on, and for a sovereign's sovereign to ride on; and for the world, familiar to us and unknown, to lay apart their particular functions and wonder at him. I once writ a sonnet in his praise and began thus: "Wonder of nature"—

Orl.   I have heard a sonnet begin so to one's mistress.

Dau.   Then did they imitate that which I composed to my courser; for my horse is my mistress.

Orl.   Your mistress bears well.

Dau.   Me well; which is the prescript praise and perfection of a good and particular mistress.

Con.   Nay, for methought yesterday your mistress shrewdly shook your back.

Dau.   So perhaps did yours.

Con.   Mine was not bridled.

Dau.   O! then belike she was old and gentle; and you rode, like a kern of Ireland, your French hose off, and in your strait strossers.

Con.   You have good judgment in horsemanship.

Dau.   Be warned by me, then: they that ride so, and ride

"What a long night is this! Will it never be morning?"

not warily, fall into foul bogs. I had rather have my horse to my mistress.

Con.   I had as lief have my mistress a jade.

Dau.   I tell thee, constable, my mistress wears his own hair.

Con.   I could make as true a boast as that if I had a sow to my mistress.

Dau.   *Le chien est retourné a son propre vomissement, et la truie lavée au bourbier:* thou makest use of any thing.

Con.   Yet do I not use my horse for my mistress; or any such proverb so little kin to the purpose.

Ram.   My lord constable, the armour that I saw in your tent to-night, are those stars or suns upon it?

Con.   Stars, my lord.

Dau.   Some of them will fall to-morrow, I hope.

Con.   And yet my sky shall not want.

Dau.   That may be, for you bear a many superfluously, and 'twere more honour some were away.

Con.   Even as your horse bears your praises; who would trot as well were some of your brags dismounted.

Dau.   Would I were able to load him with his desert! Will it never be day? I will trot to-morrow a mile, and my way shall be paved with English faces.

Con.   I will not say so for fear I should be faced out of my way. But I would it were morning, for I would fain be about the ears of the English.

Ram.   Who will go to hazard with me for twenty prisoners?

Con.   You must first go yourself to hazard, ere you have them.

Dau.   'Tis midnight; I'll go arm myself.   [*Exit.*

Orl.   The Dauphin longs for morning.

Ram.   He longs to eat the English.

Con. I think he will eat all he kills.

Orl. By the white hand of my lady, he's a gallant prince.

Con. Swear by her foot, that she may tread out the oath.

Orl. He is simply the most active gentleman of France.

Con. Doing is activity, and he will still be doing.

Orl. He never did harm, that I heard of.

Con. Nor will do none to-morrow: he will keep that good name still.

Orl. I know him to be valiant.

Con. I was told that by one that knows him better than you.

Orl. What's he?

Con. Marry, he told me so himself; and he said he cared not who knew it.

Orl. He needs not; it is no hidden virtue in him.

Con. By my faith, sir, but it is; never any body saw it but his lackey: 'tis a hooded valour; and when it appears, it will bate.

Orl. Ill will never said well.

Con. I will cap that proverb with "There is flattery in friendship."

Orl. And I will take up that with "Give the devil his due."

Con. Well placed: there stands your friend for the devil: have at the very eye of that proverb with "A pox of the devil."

Orl. You are the better at proverbs, by how much "A fool's bolt is soon shot."

Con. You have shot over.

Orl. 'Tis not the first time you were overshot.

Enter a Messenger.

Mess.   My lord high constable, the English lie within fifteen hundred paces of your tents.

Con.   Who hath measured the ground?

Mess.   The Lord Grandpré.

Con.   A valiant and most expert gentleman. Would it were day! Alas! poor Harry of England, he longs not for the dawning as we do.

Orl.   What a wretched and peevish fellow is this king of England, to mope with his fat-brained followers so far out of his knowledge!

Con.   If the English had any apprehension, they would run away.

Orl.   That they lack; for if their heads had any intellectual armour, they could never wear such heavy head-pieces.

Ram.   That island of England breeds very valiant creatures; their mastiffs are of unmatchable courage.

Orl.   Foolish curs! that run winking into the mouth of a Russian bear and have their heads crushed like rotten apples. You may as well say that's a valiant flea that dare eat his breakfast on the lip of a lion.

Con.   Just, just; and the men do sympathize with the mastiffs in robustious and rough coming on, leaving their wits with their wives: and then give them great meals of beef and iron and steel, they will eat like wolves and fight like devils.

Orl.   Ay, but these English are shrewdly out of beef.

Con.   Then shall we find to-morrow they have only stomachs to eat and none to fight. Now is it time to arm; come, shall we about it?

Orl.   It is now two o'clock: but, let me see, by ten
We shall have each a hundred Englishmen.   [*Exeunt.*

ACT IV

Enter CHORUS.

Now entertain conjecture of a time
When creeping murmur and the poring dark
Fills the wide vessel of the universe.
From camp to camp through the foul womb of night
The hum of either army stilly sounds,
That the fix'd sentinels almost receive
The secret whispers of each other's watch:
Fire answers fire, and through their paly flames
Each battle sees the other's umber'd face;
Steed threatens steed, in high and boastful neighs
Piercing the night's dull ear; and from the tents
The armourers, accomplishing the knights,
With busy hammers closing rivets up,
Give dreadful note of preparation.
The country's cocks do crow, the clocks do toll,
And the third hour of drowsy morning name.
Proud of their numbers, and secure in soul,
The confident and over-lusty French
Do the low-rated English play at dice;
And chide the cripple tardy-gaited night
Who, like a foul and ugly witch, doth limp
So tediously away. The poor condemned English,
Like sacrifices, by their watchful fires
Sit patiently, and inly ruminate
The morning's danger, and their gesture sad
Investing lank-lean cheeks and war-worn coats
Presenteth them unto the gazing moon
So many horrid ghosts. O! now, who will behold

"A little touch of Harry in the night"

Act IV Prologue

The royal captain of this ruin'd band
Walking from watch to watch, from tent to tent,
Let him cry "Praise and glory on his head!"
For forth he goes and visits all his host,
Bids them good-morrow with a modest smile,
And calls them brothers, friends and countrymen.
Upon his royal face there is no note
How dread an army hath enrounded him;
Nor doth he dedicate one jot of colour
Unto the weary and all-watched night;
But freshly looks and overbears attaint
With cheerful semblance and sweet majesty;
That every wretch, pining and pale before,
Beholding him, plucks comfort from his looks.
A largess universal like the sun
His liberal eye doth give to every one,
Thawing cold fear, that mean and gentle all,
Behold, as may unworthiness define,
A little touch of Harry in the night.
And so our scene must to the battle fly;
Where, O for pity! we shall much disgrace
With four or five most vile and ragged foils,
Right ill-dispos'd in brawl ridiculous,
The name of Agincourt. Yet sit and see;
Minding true things by what their mockeries be.

[*Exit.*

SCENE I.—*The English Camp at Agincourt.*
Enter KING HENRY, BEDFORD, *and* GLOUCESTER.

K. Hen.   Gloucester, 'tis true that we are in great danger;
The greater therefore should our courage be.
Good morrow, brother Bedford. God Almighty!
There is some soul of goodness in things evil,
Would men observingly distil it out;
For our bad neighbour makes us early stirrers,
Which is both healthful and good husbandry:
Besides, they are our outward consciences,
And preachers to us all; admonishing
That we should dress us fairly for our end.
Thus may we gather honey from the weed,
And make a moral of the devil himself.

Enter ERPINGHAM.

Good morrow, old Sir Thomas Erpingham:
A good soft pillow for that good white head
Were better than a churlish turf of France.

Erp.   Not so, my liege: this lodging likes me better,
Since I may say "Now lie I like a king."

K. Hen.   'Tis good for men to love their present pains
Upon example; so the spirit is eased:
And when the mind is quicken'd, out of doubt,
The organs, though defunct and dead before,
Break up their drowsy grave, and newly move
With casted slough and fresh legerity.
Lend me thy cloak, Sir Thomas. Brothers both,
Commend me to the princes in our camp;
Do my good-morrow to them; and anon
Desire them all to my pavilion.

Glou.   We shall, my liege.

Erp.   Shall I attend your grace?

K. Hen.   No, my good knight;
     Go with my brothers to my lords of England:
     I and my bosom must debate awhile,
     And then I would no other company.

Erp.   The Lord in heaven bless thee, noble Harry!

                                        [*Exeunt all but King.*

K. Hen.   God-a-mercy, old heart! thou speak'st cheerfully.

                    Enter PISTOL.

Pist.   *Qui va là?*

K. Hen.   A friend.

Pist.   Discuss unto me; art thou officer?
     Or art thou base, common and popular?

K. Hen.   I am a gentleman of a company.

Pist.   Trail'st thou the puissant pike?

K. Hen.   Even so. What are you?

Pist.   As good a gentleman as the emperor.

K. Hen.   Then you are a better than the king.

Pist.   The king's a bawcock, and a heart of gold,
     A lad of life, an imp of fame;
     Of parents good, of fist most valiant:
     I kiss his dirty shoe, and from heart-string
     I love the lovely bully. What is thy name?

K. Hen.   Harry le Roy.

Pist.   Le Roy! a Cornish name: art thou of Cornish crew?

K. Hen.   No, I am a Welshman.

Pist.   Know'st thou Fluellen?

K. Hen.   Yes.

Pist.   Tell him, I'll knock his leek about his pate
     Upon Saint Davy's day.

K. Hen.   Do not you wear your dagger in your cap that
day, lest he knock that about yours.

Pist.   Art thou his friend?

K. Hen.   And his kinsman too.

Pist.   The figo for thee then!

K. Hen.   I thank you. God be with you!

Pist.   My name is Pistol called.

K. Hen.   It sorts well with your fierceness.

Enter FLUELLEN *and* GOWER.

Gow.   Captain Fluellen!

Flu.   So! in the name of Jesu Christ, speak lower. It is the
greatest admiration in the universal world, when the true
and aunchient prerogatifes and laws of the wars is not
kept. If you would take the pains but to examine the
wars of Pompey the Great, you shall find, I warrant you,
that there is no tiddle taddle nor pibble pabble in Pompey's camp; I warrant you, you shall find the ceremonies
of the wars, and the cares of it, and the forms of it, and
the sobriety of it, and the modesty of it, to be otherwise.

Gow.   Why, the enemy is loud; you hear him all night.

Flu.   If the enemy is an ass and a fool and a prating coxcomb, is it meet, think you, that we should also, look
you, be an ass and a fool and a prating coxcomb? in your
own conscience now?

Gow.   I will speak lower.

Flu.   I pray you and beseech you that you will.

[*Exeunt Gower and Fluellen.*

K. Hen.   Though it appear a little out of fashion,
There is much care and valour in this Welshman.

Enter three soldiers, JOHN BATES, ALEXANDER COURT, *and*
MICHAEL WILLIAMS.

Court. Brother John Bates, is not that the morning which breaks yonder?

Bates. I think it be; but we have no great cause to desire the approach of day.

Will. We see yonder the beginning of the day, but I think we shall never see the end of it. Who goes there?

K. Hen. A friend.

Will. Under what captain serve you?

K. Hen. Under Sir Thomas Erpingham.

Will. A good old commander and a most kind gentleman: I pray you, what thinks he of our estate?

K. Hen. Even as men wracked upon a sand, that look to be washed off the next tide.

Bates. He hath not told his thought to the king?

K. Hen. No; nor it is not meet he should. For, though I speak it to you, I think the king is but a man, as I am: the violet smells to him as it doth to me; the element shows to him as it doth to me; all his senses have but human conditions: his ceremonies laid by, in his nakedness he appears but a man; and though his affections are higher mounted than ours, yet when they stoop, they stoop with the like wing. Therefore when he sees reason of fears, as we do, his fears, out of doubt, be of the same relish as ours are: yet, in reason, no man should possess him with any appearance of fear, lest he, by showing it, should dishearten his army.

Bates. He may show what outward courage he will, but I believe, as cold a night as 'tis, he could wish himself in

Thames up to the neck, and so I would he were, and I by him, at all adventures, so we were quit here.

K. Hen. By my troth, I will speak my conscience of the king: I think he would not wish himself any where but where he is.

Bates. Then I would he were here alone; so should he be sure to be ransomed, and a many poor men's lives saved.

K. Hen. I dare say you love him not so ill to wish him here alone, howsoever you speak this to feel other men's minds: methinks I could not die any where so contented as in the king's company, his cause being just and his quarrel honourable.

Will. That's more than we know.

Bates. Ay, or more than we should seek after; for we know enough if we know we are the king's subjects. If his cause be wrong, our obedience to the king wipes the crime of it out of us.

Will. But if the cause be not good, the king himself hath a heavy reckoning to make; when all those legs and arms and heads, chopped off in a battle, shall join together at the latter day, and cry all "We died at such a place"; some swearing, some crying for a surgeon, some upon their wives left poor behind them, some upon the debts they owe, some upon their children rawly left. I am afeard there are few die well that die in a battle; for how can they charitably dispose of any thing when blood is their argument? Now, if these men do not die well, it will be a black matter for the king that led them to it, who to disobey were against all proportion of subjection.

K. Hen. So, if a son that is by his father sent about merchandise do sinfully miscarry upon the sea, the imputa-

*"I will speak my conscience of the king: I think he
would not wish himself any where but where he is"*

tion of his wickedness, by your rule, should be imposed upon his father that sent him: or if a servant, under his master's command transporting a sum of money, be assailed by robbers and die in many irreconciled iniquities, you may call the business of the master the author of the servant's damnation. But this is not so: the king is not bound to answer the particular endings of his soldiers, the father of his son, nor the master of his servant; for they purpose not their death when they purpose their services. Besides there is no king, be his cause never so spotless, if it come to the arbitrement of swords, can try it out with all unspotted soldiers. Some, peradventure, have on them the guilt of premeditated and contrived murder; some, of beguiling virgins with the broken seals of perjury; some, making the wars their bulwark, that have before gored the gentle bosom of peace with pillage and robbery. Now, if these men have defeated the law and outrun native punishment, though they can outstrip men, they have no wings to fly from God: war is his beadle, war is his vengeance; so that here men are punished for before-breach of the king's laws in now the king's quarrel: where they feared the death they have borne life away, and where they would be safe they perish. Then, if they die unprovided, no more is the king guilty of their damnation than he was before guilty of those impieties for the which they are now visited. Every subject's duty is the king's; but every subject's soul is his own. Therefore should every soldier in the wars do as every sick man in his bed, wash every mote out of his conscience; and dying so, death is to him advantage; or not dying, the time was blessedly lost wherein such preparation was gained: and in him that escapes, it were not sin to think that, making God so free an offer, he let him outlive that day to see his greatness, and to teach others how they should prepare.

Will. 'Tis certain, every man that dies ill, the ill upon his own head; the king is not to answer it.

Bates. I do not desire he should answer for me; and yet I determine to fight lustily for him.

K. Hen. I myself heard the king say he would not be ransomed.

Will. Ay, he said so, to make us fight cheerfully; but when our throats are cut he may be ransomed, and we ne'er the wiser.

K. Hen. If I live to see it, I will never trust his word after.

Will. You pay him then. That's a perilous shot out of an elder-gun, that a poor and a private displeasure can do against a monarch. You may as well go about to turn the sun to ice with fanning in his face with a peacock's feather. You'll never trust his word after! come, 'tis a foolish saying.

K. Hen. Your reproof is something too round: I should be angry with you if the time were convenient.

Will. Let it be a quarrel between us, if you live.

K. Hen. I embrace it.

Will. How shall I know thee again?

K. Hen. Give me any gage of thine, and I will wear it in my bonnet: then, if ever thou darest acknowledge it, I will make it my quarrel.

Will. Here's my glove: give me another of thine.

K. Hen. There.

Will. This will I also wear in my cap: if ever thou come to me and say after to-morrow, "This is my glove," by this hand I will take thee a box on the ear.

K. Hen.   If ever I live to see it, I will challenge it.

Will.   Thou darest as well be hanged.

K. Hen.   Well, I will do it, though I take thee in the king's company.

Will.   Keep thy word: fare thee well.

Bates.   Be friends, you English fools, be friends: we have French quarrels enow, if you could tell how to reckon.

K. Hen.   Indeed, the French may lay twenty French crowns to one, they will beat us; for they bear them on their shoulders: but it is no English treason to cut French crowns, and to-morrow the king himself will be a clipper.   [*Exeunt Soldiers.*

Upon the king! let us our lives, our souls,
Our debts, our careful wives,
Our children, and our sins lay on the king!
We must bear all. O hard condition!
Twin-born with greatness, subject to the breath
Of every fool, whose sense no more can feel
But his own wringing. What infinite heart's ease
Must kings neglect that private men enjoy!
And what have kings that privates have not too,
Save ceremony, save general ceremony?
And what art thou, thou idol ceremony?
What kind of god art thou, that suffer'st more
Of mortal griefs than do thy worshippers?
What are thy rents? what are thy comings-in?
O ceremony, show me but thy worth!
What is thy soul of adoration?
Art thou aught else but place, degree, and form,

Creating awe and fear in other men?
Wherein thou art less happy, being fear'd,
Than they in fearing.
What drink'st thou oft, instead of homage sweet,
But poison'd flattery? O! be sick, great greatness,
And bid thy ceremony give thee cure.
Think'st thou the fiery fever will go out
With titles blown from adulation?
Will it give place to flexure and low-bending?
Canst thou, when thou command'st the beggar's knee,
Command the health of it? No, thou proud dream,
That play'st so subtly with a king's repose;
I am a king that find thee; and I know
'Tis not the balm, the sceptre and the ball,
The sword, the mace, the crown imperial,
The intertissued robe of gold and pearl,
The farced title running 'fore the king,
The throne he sits on, nor the tide of pomp
That beats upon the high shore of this world,
No, not all these, thrice-gorgeous ceremony,
Not all these, laid in bed majestical,
Can sleep so soundly as the wretched slave,
Who with a body fill'd and vacant mind
Gets him to rest, cramm'd with distressful bread;
Never sees horrid night, the child of hell,
But, like a lackey, from the rise to set
Sweats in the eye of Phœbus, and all night
Sleeps in Elysium; next day after dawn,
Doth rise and help Hyperion to his horse,
And follows so the ever-running year
With profitable labour to his grave:

"My lord, your nobles, jealous of your absence,
Seek through your camp to find you"

And, but for ceremony, such a wretch,
Winding up days with toil and nights with sleep,
Had the fore-hand and vantage of a king.
The slave, a member of the country's peace,
Enjoys it; but in gross brain little wots
What watch the king keeps to maintain the peace,
Whose hours the peasant best advantages.

Enter ERPINGHAM.

Erp.   My lord, your nobles, jealous of your absence,
Seek through your camp to find you.

K. Hen.   Good old knight,
Collect them all together at my tent:
I'll be before thee.

Erp.   I shall do 't, my lord.   [*Exit.*

K. Hen.   O God of battles! steel my soldiers' hearts;
Possess them not with fear; take from them now
The sense of reckoning, if the opposed numbers
Pluck their hearts from them. Not to-day, O Lord!
O! not to-day, think not upon the fault
My father made in compassing the crown.
I Richard's body have interred new,
And on it have bestow'd more contrite tears
Than from it issued forced drops of blood.
Five hundred poor I have in yearly pay,
Who twice a day their wither'd hands hold up
Toward heaven, to pardon blood; and I have built
Two chantries, where the sad and solemn priests
Sing still for Richard's soul. More will I do;
Though all that I can do is nothing worth,
Since that my penitence comes after all,
Imploring pardon.

Enter GLOUCESTER.

Enter GLOUCESTER.

Glou.   My liege!
K. Hen.   My brother Gloucester's voice! Ay;
I know thy errand, I will go with thee:
The day, my friends, and all things stay for me.

[Exeunt.

SCENE II.—*The French Camp.*

Enter the DAUPHIN, ORLEANS, RAMBURES, *and others.*

Orl.   The sun doth gild our armour; up, my lords!
Dau.   *Montez à cheval!* My horse! *valet! lacquais!* ha!
Orl.   O brave spirit!
Dau.   *Via! les eaux et la terre!*
Orl.   *Rien puis? l'air et le feu!*
Dau.   *Ciel!* cousin Orleans.

Enter Constable.

Now, my lord constable!
Con.   Hark, how our steeds for present service neigh!
Dau.   Mount them, and make incision in their hides,
That their hot blood may spin in English eyes,
And dout them with superfluous courage, ha!
Ram.   What! will you have them weep our horses' blood?
How shall we then behold their natural tears?

Enter Messenger.

Mess.   The English are embattail'd, you French peers.
Con.   To horse, you gallant princes! straight to horse!
Do but behold yon poor and starved band,
And your fair show shall suck away their souls,
Leaving them but the shales and husks of men.
There is not work enough for all our hands;

Scarce blood enough in all their sickly veins
To give each naked curtle-axe a stain,
That our French gallants shall to-day draw out,
And sheathe for lack of sport: let us but blow on them,
The vapour of our valour will o'erturn them.
'Tis positive 'gainst all exceptions, lords,
That our superfluous lackeys and our peasants,
Who in unnecessary action swarm
About our squares of battle, were enow
To purge this field of such a hilding foe,
Though we upon this mountain's basis by
Took stand for idle speculation:
But that our honours must not. What's to say?
A very little little let us do,
And all is done. Then let the trumpets sound
The tucket sonance and the note to mount:
For our approach shall so much dare the field
That England shall couch down in fear, and yield.

Enter GRANDPRÉ.

Grand.   Why do you stay so long, my lords of France?
Yon island carrions, desperate of their bones,
Ill-favour'dly become the morning field:
Their ragged curtains poorly are let loose,
And our air shakes them passing scornfully:
Big Mars seems bankrupt in their beggar'd host,
And faintly through a rusty beaver peeps:
The horsemen sit like fixed candlesticks,
With torch-staves in their hand; and their poor jades
Lob down their heads, dropping the hides and hips,
The gum down-roping from their pale-dead eyes,

And in their pale dull mouths the gimmal'd bit
Lies foul with chaw'd grass, still and motionless;
And their executors, the knavish crows,
Fly o'er them, all impatient for their hour.
Description cannot suit itself in words
To demonstrate the life of such a battle
In life so lifeless as it shows itself.

Con.   They have said their prayers, and they stay for death.

Dau.   Shall we go send them dinners and fresh suits,
And give their fasting horses provender,
And after fight with them?

Con.   I stay but for my guard. On to the field!
I will the banner from a trumpet take,
And use it for my haste. Come, come, away!
The sun is high, and we outwear the day.   [*Exeunt.*

SCENE III.—*The English camp.*

Enter GLOUCESTER, BEDFORD, EXETER, ERPINGHAM, *with
all his host;* SALISBURY, *and* WESTMORELAND.

Glou.   Where is the king?

Bed.   The king himself is rode to view their battle.

West.   Of fighting men they have full threescore thousand.

Exe.   There's five to one; besides, they all are fresh.

Sal.   God's arm strike with us! 'tis a fearful odds.
God be wi' you, princes all; I 'll to my charge:
If we no more meet till we meet in heaven,
Then, joyfully, my noble Lord of Bedford,
My dear Lord Gloucester, and my good Lord Exeter,
And my kind kinsman, warriors all, adieu!

Bed.   Farewell, good Salisbury; and good luck go with
thee!

Exe.   Farewell, kind lord. Fight valiantly to-day:
    And yet I do thee wrong to mind thee of it,
    For thou art fram'd of the firm truth of valour.

                                  [Exit Salisbury.

Bed.   He is as full of valour as of kindness;
    Princely in both.

Enter the King.

West.   O! that we now had here
    But one ten thousand of those men in England
    That do no work to-day.

K. Hen.   What's he that wishes so?
    My cousin Westmoreland? No, my fair cousin:
    If we are mark'd to die, we are enow
    To do our country loss; and if to live,
    The fewer men, the greater share of honour.
    God's will! I pray thee, wish not one man more.
    By Jove, I am not covetous for gold,
    Nor care I who doth feed upon my cost;
    It yearns me not if men my garments wear;
    Such outward things dwell not in my desires:
    But if it be a sin to covet honour,
    I am the most offending soul alive.
    No, faith, my coz, wish not a man from England:
    God's peace! I would not lose so great an honour
    As one man more, methinks, would share from me,
    For the best hope I have. O! do not wish one more:
    Rather proclaim it, Westmoreland, through my host,
    That he which hath no stomach to this fight,
    Let him depart; his passport shall be made,
    And crowns for convoy put into his purse:

We would not die in that man's company
That fears his fellowship to die with us.
This day is call'd the feast of Crispian:
He that outlives this day, and comes safe home,
Will stand a tip-toe when this day is nam'd,
And rouse him at the name of Crispian.
He that shall live this day, and see old age,
Will yearly on the vigil feast his neighbours,
And say "To-morrow is Saint Crispian":
Then will he strip his sleeve and show his scars,
And say "These wounds I had on Crispin's day."
Old men forget; yet all shall be forgot,
But he'll remember with advantages
What feats he did that day. Then shall our names,
Familiar in his mouth as household words,
Harry the king, Bedford and Exeter,
Warwick and Talbot, Salisbury and Gloucester,
Be in their flowing cups freshly remember'd.
This story shall the good man teach his son;
And Crispin Crispian shall ne'er go by,
From this day to the ending of the world,
But we in it shall be remembered;
We few, we happy few, we band of brothers;
For he to-day that sheds his blood with me
Shall be my brother; be he ne'er so vile
This day shall gentle his condition:
And gentlemen in England now a-bed
Shall think themselves accurs'd they were not here,
And hold their manhoods cheap whiles any speaks
That fought with us upon Saint Crispin's day.

"*The French are bravely in their battles set
And will with all expedience charge on us*"

Re-enter SALISBURY.

Sal.   My sovereign lord, bestow yourself with speed:
The French are bravely in their battles set,
And will with all expedience charge on us.

K. Hen.   All things are ready, if our minds be so.

West.   Perish the man whose mind is backward now!

K. Hen.   Thou dost not wish more help from England, coz?

West.   God's will! my liege, would you and I alone,
Without more help, could fight this royal battle!

K. Hen.   Why, now thou hast unwish'd five thousand men;
Which likes me better than to wish us one.
You know your places: God be with you all!

Tucket. Enter MONTJOY.

Mont.   Once more I come to know of thee, King Harry,
If for thy ransom thou wilt now compound,
Before thy most assured overthrow:
For certainly thou art so near the gulf
Thou needs must be englutted. Besides, in mercy,
The constable desires thee thou wilt mind
Thy followers of repentance; that their souls
May make a peaceful and a sweet retire
From off these fields, where, wretches, their poor bodies
Must lie and fester.

K. Hen.   Who hath sent thee now?

Mont.   The Constable of France.

K. Hen.   I pray thee, bear my former answer back:
Bid them achieve me and then sell my bones.
Good God! why should they mock poor fellows thus?
The man that once did sell the lion's skin
While the beast liv'd, was kill'd with hunting him.

A many of our bodies shall no doubt
Find native graves; upon the which, I trust,
Shall witness live in brass of this day's work;
And those that leave their valiant bones in France,
Dying like men, though buried in your dunghills,
They shall be fam'd; for there the sun shall greet them,
And draw their honours reeking up to heaven,
Leaving their earthly parts to choke your clime,
The smell whereof shall breed a plague in France.
Mark then abounding valour in our English,
That being dead, like to the bullet's grazing,
Break out into a second course of mischief,
Killing in relapse of mortality.
Let me speak proudly: tell the constable
We are but warriors for the working-day;
Our gayness and our gilt are all besmirch'd
With rainy marching in the painful field;
There's not a piece of feather in our host—
Good argument, I hope, we will not fly—
And time hath worn us into slovenry:
But, by the mass, our hearts are in the trim;
And my poor soldiers tell me, yet ere night
They 'll be in fresher robes, or they will pluck
The gay new coats o'er the French soldiers' heads,
And turn them out of service. If they do this,
As, if God please, they shall, my ransom then
Will soon be levied. Herald, save thou thy labour;
Come thou no more for ransom, gentle herald:
They shall have none, I swear, but these my joints;
Which if they have as I will leave 'em them,
Shall yield them little, tell the constable.

Mont.   I shall, King Harry. And so fare thee well:
Thou never shalt hear herald any more.   [*Exit.*

K. Hen.   I fear thou wilt once more come again for a
ransom.

Enter YORK.

York.   My lord, most humbly on my knee I beg
The leading of the vaward.

K. Hen.   Take it, brave York. Now, soldiers, march away:
And how thou pleasest, God, dispose the day!

[*Exeunt.*

SCENE IV.—*The Field of Battle.*

Alarums. Excursions. Enter PISTOL, *French Soldier, and Boy.*

Pist.   Yield, cur!

Fr. Sold.   *Je pense que vous estes gentilhomme de bonne qualité.*

Pist.   *Qualtitie calmie custure me!* Art thou a gentleman?
What is thy name? discuss.

Fr. Sold.   *O Seigneur Dieu!*

Pist.   O, Signieur Dew should be a gentleman:
Perpend my words, O Signieur Dew, and mark:
O Signieur Dew, thou diest on point of fox,
Except, O signieur, thou do give to me
Egregious ransom.

Fr. Sold.   *O, prenez miséricorde! ayez pitié de moy!*

Pist.   Moy shall not serve; I will have forty moys;
Or I will fetch thy rim out at thy throat
In drops of crimson blood.

Fr. Sold.   *Est il impossible d'eschapper la force de ton bras?*

Pist.   Brass, cur!
Thou damned and luxurious mountain goat,
Offer'st me brass?

Fr. Sold.   *O pardonnez moy!*

Pist.   Say'st thou me so? is that a ton of moys?
Come hither, boy
Ask me this slave in French
What is his name.

Boy.   *Escoutez: comment estes vous appellé?*

Fr. Sold.   *Monsieur le Fer.*

Boy.   He says his name is Master Fer.

Pist.   Master Fer! I'll fer him, and firk him, and ferret him.
Discuss the same in French unto him.

Boy.   I do not know the French for fer, and ferret, and firk.

Pist.   Bid him prepare, for I will cut his throat.

Fr. Sold.   *Que dit-il, monsieur?*

Boy.   *Il me commande à vous dire que vous faites vous prest; car
ce soldat icy est disposé tout à cette heure de couper vostre gorge.*

Pist.   Owy, cuppele gorge, permafoy,
Peasant, unless thou give me crowns, brave crowns;
Or mangled shalt thou be by this my sword.

Fr. Sold.   *O! je vous supplie pour l'amour de Dieu, me pardonner.
Je suis gentilhomme de bonne maison: gardez ma vie, et je vous
donneray deux cents escus.*

Pist.   What are his words?

Boy.   He prays you to save his life: he is a gentleman of a
good house; and for his ransom he will give you two
hundred crowns.

Pist.   Tell him my fury shall abate, and I
The crowns will take.

Fr. Sold.   *Petit monsieur, que dit-il?*

Boy.   *Encore qu'il est contre son jurement de pardonner aucun
prisonnier; néant-moins, pour les escus que vous l'avez promis,
il est content de vous donner la liberté, le franchisement.*

"Is this the King we sent to for his ransom?"

Fr. Sold.   *Sur mes genoux je vous donne mille remerciemens; et je m'estime heureux que je suis tombé entre les mains d'un chevalier, je pense, le plus brave, vaillant, et tres-distingué seigneur d'Angleterre.*

Pist.   Expound unto me, boy.

Boy.   He gives you, upon his knees, a thousand thanks; and he esteems himself happy that he hath fallen into the hands of one, as he thinks, the most brave, valorous, and thrice-worthy signieur of England.

Pist.   As I suck blood, I will some mercy show. Follow me!

Boy.   *Suivez vous le grand capitaine.*

                    [Exeunt Pistol and French Soldier.

I did never know so full a voice issue from so empty a heart: but the saying is true, "The empty vessel makes the greatest sound." Bardolph and Nym had ten times more valour than this roaring devil i' the old play, that every one may pare his nails with a wooden dagger; and they are both hanged; and so would this be if he durst steal any thing adventurously. I must stay with the lackeys, with the luggage of our camp: the French might have a good prey of us if he knew of it; for there is none to guard it but boys.   *[Exit*

SCENE V.—*Another Part of the Field.*

Enter CONSTABLE, ORLEANS, BOURBON, DAUPHIN, *and* RAMBURES.

Con.   *O diable!*

Orl.   *O seigneur! le jour est perdu! tout est perdu!*

Dau.   *Mort de ma vie!* all is confounded, all!
     Reproach and everlasting shame
     Sits mocking in our plumes. O *meschante fortune!*
     Do not run away.   [*A short alarum.*
Con.   Why, all our ranks are broke.
Dau.   O perdurable shame! let's stab ourselves.
     Be these the wretches that we play'd at dice for?
Orl.   Is this the king we sent to for his ransom?
Bour.   Shame, and eternal shame, nothing but shame!
     Let us die in honour: once more back again;
     And he that will not follow Bourbon now,
     Let him go hence, and with his cap in hand,
     Like a base pandar, hold the chamber-door
     Whilst by a slave, no gentler than my dog,
     His fairest daughter is contaminated.
Con.   Disorder, that hath spoil'd us, friend us now!
     Let us on heaps go offer up our lives.
Orl.   We are enow yet living in the field
     To smother up the English in our throngs,
     If any order might be thought upon.
Bour.   The devil take order now! I'll to the throng:
     Let life be short, else shame will be too long.
                                                    [*Exeunt.*

SCENE VI.—*Another Part of the Field.*

Alarums. Enter KING HENRY *and Forces;* EXETER, *and others.*

K. Hen.   Well have we done, thrice-valiant countrymen:
     But all's not done; yet keep the French the field.
Exe.   The Duke of York commends him to your majesty.
K. Hen.   Lives he, good uncle? thrice within this hour
     I saw him down; thrice up again and fighting;

From helmet to the spur all blood he was.

Exe.   In which array, brave soldier, doth he lie,
Larding the plain; and by his bloody side,
Yoke-fellow to his honour-owing wounds,
The noble Earl of Suffolk also lies.
Suffolk first died; and York, all haggled over,
Comes to him, where in gore he lay insteep'd,
And takes him by the beard, kisses the gashes
That bloodily did yawn upon his face;
And cries aloud, "Tarry, dear cousin Suffolk!
My soul shall thine keep company to heaven;
Tarry, sweet soul, for mine, then fly abreast,
As in this glorious and well-foughten field
We kept together in our chivalry!"
Upon these words I came and cheer'd him up;
He smil'd me in the face, raught me his hand,
And, with a feeble gripe, says "Dear my lord,
Commend my service to my sovereign."
So did he turn, and over Suffolk's neck
He threw his wounded arm, and kiss'd his lips;
And so espous'd to death, with blood he seal'd
A testament of noble-ending love.
The pretty and sweet manner of it forc'd
Those waters from me which I would have stopp'd;
But I had not so much of man in me,
And all my mother came into mine eyes
And gave me up to tears.

K. Hen.   I blame you not;
For, hearing this, I must perforce compound
With mistful eyes, or they will issue too.   [*Alarum.*
But, hark! what new alarum is this same?

The French have reinforc'd their scatter'd men:
Then every soldier kill his prisoners!
Give the word through.   [*Exeunt.*

SCENE VII.—*Another Part of the Field.*

Enter FLUELLEN *and* GOWER.

Flu.   Kill the poys and the luggage! 'tis expressly against
the law of arms: 'tis as arrant a piece of knavery, mark
you now, as can be offer't; in your conscience now, is
it not?

Gow.   'Tis certain there's not a boy left alive; and the cowardly rascals that ran from the battle ha' done this slaughter: besides, they have burned and carried away all that
was in the king's tent; wherefore the king most worthily
hath caused every soldier to cut his prisoner's throat. O!
'tis a gallant king.

Flu.   Ay, he was porn at Monmouth, Captain Gower. What
call you the town's name where Alexander the Pig was
born?

Gow.   Alexander the Great.

Flu.   Why, I pray you, is not pig great? the pig, or the
great, or the mighty, or the huge, or the magnanimous,
are all one reckonings, save the phrase is a little varia-
tions.

Gow.   I think Alexander the Great was born in Macedon:
his father was called Philip of Macedon, as I take it.

Flu.   I think it is in Macedon where Alexander is porn. I
tell you, captain, if you look in the maps of the 'orld, I
warrant you sall find, in the comparisons between Mace-

don and Monmouth, that the situations, look you, is both alike. There is a river in Macedon, and there is also moreover a river at Monmouth: it is called Wye at Monmouth; but it is out of my prains what is the name of the other river; but 'tis all one, 'tis alike as my fingers is to my fingers, and there is salmons in both. If you mark Alexander's life well, Harry of Monmouth's life is come after it indifferent well; for there is figures in all things. Alexander, God knows, and you know, in his rages, and his furies, and his wraths, and his cholers, and his moods, and his displeasures, and his indignations, and also being a little intoxicates in his prains, did, in his ales and his angers, look you, kill his best friend, Cleitus.

Gow. Our king is not like him in that: he never killed any of his friends.

Flu. It is not well done, mark you now, to take the tales out of my mouth, ere it is made and finished. I speak but in the figures and comparisons of it: as Alexander killed his friend Cleitus, being in his ales and his cups, so also Harry Monmouth, being in his right wits and his good judgments, turned away the fat knight with the great-belly doublet: he was full of jests, and gipes, and knaveries, and mocks; I have forgot his name.

Gow. Sir John Falstaff.

Flu. That is he. I'll tell you there is good men porn at Monmouth.

Gow. Here comes his majesty.

Alarum. Enter KING HENRY *and Forces;* WARWICK, GLOUCESTER, EXETER, *and others.*

K. Hen.   I was not angry since I came to France
Until this instant. Take a trumpet, herald;
Ride thou unto the horsemen on yon hill:
If they will fight with us, bid them come down,
Or void the field; they do offend our sight.
If they'll do neither, we will come to them,
And make them skirr away, as swift as stones
Enforced from the old Assyrian slings.
Besides, we'll cut the throats of those we have,
And not a man of them that we shall take
Shall taste our mercy. Go and tell them so.

Enter MONTJOY.

Exe.   Here comes the herald of the French, my liege.
Glou.   His eyes are humbler than they used to be.
K. Hen.   How now! what means this, herald? know'st not
That I have fin'd these bones of mine for ransom?
Com'st thou again for ransom?
Mont.   No, great king:
I come to thee for charitable license,
That we may wander o'er this bloody field
To book our dead, and then to bury them;
To sort our nobles from our common men;
For many of our princes—woe the while!—
Lie drown'd and soak'd in mercenary blood;
So do our vulgar drench their peasant limbs
In blood of princes; and their wounded steeds
Fret fetlock deep in gore, and with wild rage
Yerk out their armed heels at their dead masters,

"Here comes the herald of the French, my liege.
His eyes are humbler than they used to be"

Killing them twice. O! give us leave, great king,
To view the field in safety and dispose
Of their dead bodies.

K. Hen.   I tell thee truly, herald,
I know not if the day be ours or no;
For yet a many of your horsemen peer
And gallop o'er the field.

Mont.   The day is yours.

K. Hen.   Praised be God, and not our strength, for it!
What is this castle call'd that stands hard by?

Mont.   They call it Agincourt.

K. Hen.   Then call we this the field of Agincourt,
Fought on the day of Crispin Crispianus.

Flu.   Your grandfather of famous memory, an't please your
majesty, and your great-uncle Edward the Plack Prince
of Wales, as I have read in the chronicles, fought a most
prave pattle here in France.

K. Hen.   They did, Fluellen.

Flu.   Your majesty says very true: if your majesties is remembered of it, the Welshmen did good service in a
garden where leeks did grow, wearing leeks in their
Monmouth caps; which, your majesty know, to this hour
is an honourable badge of the service; and I do believe
your majesty takes no scorn to wear the leek upon Saint
Tavy's day.

K. Hen.   I wear it for a memorable honour;
For I am Welsh, you know, good countryman.

Flu.   All the water in Wye cannot wash your majesty's
Welsh plood out of your body, I can tell you that: God
pless it and preserve it, as long as it pleases his grace, and
his majesty too!

K. Hen.   Thanks, good my countryman.

Flu.   By Jeshu, I am your majesty's countryman, I care not
who know it; I will confess it to all the 'orld: I need not
to be ashamed of your majesty, praised be God, so long
as your majesty is an honest man.

K. Hen.   God keep me so! Our heralds go with him:
Bring me just notice of the numbers dead
On both our parts. Call yonder fellow hither.

> [*Points to Williams.*
> *Exeunt Heralds with Montjoy.*

Exe.   Soldier, you must come to the king.

K. Hen.   Soldier, why wearest thou that glove in thy cap?

Will.   An't please your majesty, 'tis the gage of one that
I should fight withal, if he be alive.

K. Hen.   An Englishman?

Will.   An't please your majesty, a rascal that swaggered
with me last night; who, if alive and ever dare to challenge this glove, I have sworn to take him a box o' th'
ear: or if I can see my glove in his cap, which he swore
as he was a soldier he would wear if alive, I will strike
it out soundly.

K. Hen.   What think you, Captain Fluellen? is it fit this
soldier keep his oath?

Flu.   He is a craven and a villain else, an't please your majesty, in my conscience.

K. Hen.   It may be his enemy is a gentleman of great sort,
quite from the answer of his degree.

Flu.   Though he be as good a gentleman as the devil is, as
Lucifer and Belzebub himself, it is necessary, look your
grace, that he keep his vow and his oath. If he be per-
jured, see you now, his reputation is as arrant a villain

and a Jack-sauce as ever his black shoe trod upon God's
ground and his earth, in my conscience, la!

K. Hen.   Then keep thy vow, sirrah, when thou meetest
the fellow.

Will.   So I will, my liege, as I live.

K. Hen.   Who servest thou under?

Will.   Under Captain Gower, my liege.

Flu.   Gower is a good captain, and is good knowledge, and
literatured in the wars.

K. Hen.   Call him hither to me, soldier.

Will.   I will, my liege.   [*Exit.*

K. Hen.   Here, Fluellen; wear thou this favour for me and
stick it in thy cap. When Alençon and myself were down
together I plucked this glove from his helm: if any man
challenge this, he is a friend to Alençon, and an enemy
to our person; if thou encounter any such, apprehend
him, an thou dost me love.

Flu.   Your grace doo's me as great honours as can be de-
sired in the hearts of his subjects: I would fain see the
man that has but two legs that shall find himself ag-
griefed at this glove, that is all; but I would fain see it
once, and please God of his grace that I might see.

K. Hen.   Knowest thou Gower?

Flu.   He is my dear friend, an please you.

K. Hen.   Pray thee, go seek him, and bring him to my tent.

Flu.   I will fetch him.   [*Exit.*

K. Hen.   My Lord of Warwick, and my brother Gloucester,
Follow Fluellen closely at the heels.
The glove which I have given him for a favour
May haply purchase him a box o' th' ear;
It is the soldier's; I by bargain should

Wear it myself. Follow, good cousin Warwick:
If that the soldier strike him, as I judge
By his blunt bearing he will keep his word,
Some sudden mischief may arise of it;
For I do know Fluellen valiant,
And touch'd with choler, hot as gunpowder,
And quickly will return an injury:
Follow and see there be no harm between them.
Go you with me, uncle of Exeter.   [*Exeunt.*

SCENE VIII.—*Before King Henry's Pavilion.*

Enter GOWER *and* WILLIAMS.

Will.   I warrant it is to knight you, captain.

Enter FLUELLEN.

Flu.   God's will and his pleasure, captain, I beseech you
now come apace to the king: there is more good toward
you peradventure than is in your knowledge to dream of.

Will.   Sir, know you this glove?

Flu.   Know the glove! I know the glove is a glove.

Will.   I know this; and thus I challenge it.   [*Strikes him.*

Flu.   'Sblood! an arrant traitor as any's in the universal
world, or in France, or in England.

Gow.   How now, sir! you villain!

Will.   Do you think I'll be forsworn?

Flu.   Stand away, Captain Gower: I will give treason his
payment into plows, I warrant you.

Will.   I am no traitor.

Flu.   That's a lie in thy throat. I charge you in his majesty's
name, apprehend him: he's a friend of the Duke Alençon's.

"This note doth tell me of ten thousand French
That in the field lie slain"

Enter WARWICK *and* GLOUCESTER.

War.   How now, how now! what's the matter?

Flu.   My Lord of Warwick, here is, praised be God for it! a most contagious treason come to light, look you, as you shall desire in a summer's day. Here is his majesty.

Enter KING HENRY *and* EXETER.

K. Hen.   How now! what's the matter?

Flu.   My liege, here is a villain and a traitor, that, look your grace, has struck the glove which your majesty is take out of the helmet of Alençon.

Will.   My liege, this was my glove; here is the fellow of it; and he that I gave it to in change promised to wear it in his cap: I promised to strike him if he did. I met this man with my glove in his cap, and I have been as good as my word.

Flu.   Your majesty hear now, saving your majesty's manhood, what an arrant, rascally, beggarly, lousy knave it is. I hope your majesty is pear me testimony and witness, and will avouchment that this is the glove of Alençon that your majesty is give me; in your conscience now?

K. Hen.   Give me thy glove, soldier: look, here is the fellow of it.
'Twas I, indeed, thou promised'st to strike;
And thou hast given me most bitter terms.

Flu.   An please your majesty, let his neck answer for it, if there is any martial law in the world.

K. Hen.   How canst thou make me satisfaction?

Will.   All offences, my lord, come from the heart: never came any from mine that might offend your majesty.

K. Hen.   It was ourself thou didst abuse.

Will.　Your majesty came not like yourself: you appeared to me but as a common man; witness the night, your garments, your lowliness; and what your highness suffered under that shape, I beseech you, take it for your own fault and not mine: for had you been as I took you for, I made no offence; therefore, I beseech your highness, pardon me.

K. Hen.　Here, uncle Exeter, fill this glove with crowns, And give it to this fellow. Keep it, fellow; And wear it for an honour in thy cap Till I do challenge it. Give him the crowns. And, captain, you must needs be friends with him.

Flu.　By this day and this light, the fellow has mettle enough in his belly. Hold, there is twelve pence for you, and I pray you to serve God, and keep you out of prawls, and prabbles, and quarrels, and dissensions, and, I warrant you, it is the better for you.

Will.　I will none of your money.

Flu.　It is with a good will; I can tell you it will serve you to mend your shoes: come, wherefore should you be so pashful? your shoes is not so good: 'tis a good silling, I warrant you, or I will change it.

Enter an English Herald.

K. Hen.　Now, herald, are the dead numbered?

Her.　Here is the number of the slaughter'd French.

　　　　　　　　　　　　[Kneeling and delivering papers.

K. Hen.　What prisoners of good sort are taken, uncle?

Exe.　Charles Duke of Orleans, nephew to the king; John Duke of Bourbon, and Lord Bouciqualt: Of other lords and barons, knights and squires,

Full fifteen hundred, besides common men.

K. Hen.   This note doth tell me of ten thousand French
That in the field lie slain: of princes, in this number,
And nobles bearing banners, there lie dead
One hundred twenty-six: added to these,
Of knights, esquires, and gallant gentlemen,
Eight thousand and four hundred; of the which
Five hundred were but yesterday dubb'd knights:
So that, in these ten thousand they have lost,
There are but sixteen hundred mercenaries;
The rest are princes, barons, lords, knights, squires,
And gentlemen of blood and quality.
The names of those their nobles that lie dead:
Charles Delabreth, high constable of France;
Jacques of Chatillon, admiral of France;
The master of the cross-bows, Lord Rambures;
Great Master of France, the brave Sir Guichard
   Dauphin;
John Duke of Alençon; Anthony Duke of Brabant,
The brother to the Duke of Burgundy;
And Edward Duke of Bar: of lusty earls,
Grandpré and Roussi, Fauconberg and Foix,
Beaumont and Marle, Vaudemont and Lestrale.
Here was a royal fellowship of death!
Where is the number of our English dead?

              [Herald shows him another paper.

Edward the Duke of York, the Earl of Suffolk,
Sir Richard Ketly, Davy Gam, esquire:
None else of name; and of all other men
But five and twenty. O God! thy arm was here;
And not to us, but to thy arm alone,

Ascribe we all. When, without stratagem,
But in plain shock and even play of battle,
Was ever known so great and little loss
On one part and on the other? Take it, God,
For it is none but thine!

Exe.   'Tis wonderful!

K. Hen.   Come, go we in procession to the village:
And be it death proclaimed through our host
To boast of this or take that praise from God
Which is his only.

Flu.   Is it not lawful, an please your majesty, to tell how
many is killed?

K. Hen.   Yes, captain; but with this acknowledgment,
That God fought for us.

Flu.   Yes, my conscience, he did us great good.

K. Hen.   Do we all holy rites:
Let there be sung "*Non nobis*" and "*Te Deum*";
The dead with charity enclos'd in clay.
And then to Calais; and to England then;
Where ne'er from France arriv'd more happy men.

                       [*Exeunt.*

ACT V

Enter CHORUS.

Vouchsafe to those that have not read the story,
That I may prompt them: and of such as have,
I humbly pray them to admit the excuse
Of time, of numbers, and due course of things,
Which cannot in their huge and proper life
Be here presented. Now we bear the king
Toward Calais: grant him there; there seen,

Heave him away upon your winged thoughts
Athwart the sea. Behold, the English beach
Pales in the flood with men, with wives, and boys,
Whose shouts and claps out-voice the deep-mouth'd sea,
Which, like a mighty whiffler, 'fore the king
Seems to prepare his way: so let him land,
And solemnly see him set on to London.
So swift a pace hath thought that even now
You may imagine him upon Blackheath;
Where that his lords desire him to have borne
His bruised helmet and his bended sword
Before him through the city: he forbids it,
Being free from vainness and self-glorious pride;
Giving full trophy, signal and ostent,
Quite from himself, to God. But now behold,
In the quick forge and working-house of thought,
How London doth pour out her citizens.
The mayor and all his brethren in best sort,
Like to the senators of the antique Rome,
With the plebeians swarming at their heels,
Go forth and fetch their conquering Cæsar in:
As, by a lower, but by loving likelihood,
Were now the general of our gracious empress,
As in good time he may, from Ireland coming,
Bringing rebellion broached on his sword,
How many would the peaceful city quit
To welcome him! much more, and much more cause,
Did they this Harry. Now in London place him;
As yet the lamentation of the French
Invites the King of England's stay at home;
The emperor's coming in behalf of France,

To order peace between them; and omit
All the occurrences, whatever chanc'd,
Till Harry's back-return again to France:
There must we bring him; and myself have play'd
The interim, by remembering you 'tis past.
Then brook abridgement, and your eyes advance,
After your thoughts, straight back again to France.

[*Exit.*

SCENE I.—*France. The English Camp.*

Enter FLUELLEN *and* GOWER.

Gow. Nay, that's right; but why wear you your leek to-day? Saint Davy's day is past.

Flu. There is occasions and causes why and wherefore in all things: I will tell you, asse my friend, Captain Gower. The rascally, scauld, beggarly, lousy, pragging knave, Pistol, which you and yourself and all the world know to be no petter than a fellow, look you now, of no merits, he is come to me and prings me pread and salt yesterday, look you, and bid me eat my leek. It was in a place where I could not breed no contention with him; but I will be so bold as to wear it in my cap till I see him once again, and then I will tell him a little piece of my desires.

Enter PISTOL.

Gow. Why, here he comes, swelling like a turkey-cock.

Flu. 'Tis no matter for his swellings nor his turkey-cocks. God pless you, Aunchient Pistol! you scurvy, lousy knave, God pless you!

Pist. Ha! art thou bedlam? dost thou thirst, base Trojan To have me fold up Parca's fatal web?
Hence! I am qualmish at the smell of leek.

"*I pray you, fall to: if you can mock a leek,
you can eat a leek*"

Flu. I peseech you heartily, scurvy lousy knave, at my desires and my requests and my petitions to eat, look you, this leek; because, look you, you do not love it, nor your affections and your appetites and your digestions doo's not agree with it, I would desire you to eat it.

Pist. Not for Cadwallader and all his goats.

Flu. There is one goat for you. [*Strikes him.*] Will you be so good, scauld knave, as eat it?

Pist. Base Trojan, thou shalt die.

Flu. You say very true, scauld knave, when God's will is. I will desire you to live in the mean time and eat your victuals: come, there is sauce for it. [*Strikes him.*] You called me yesterday mountain-squire, but I will make you to-day a squire of low degree. I pray you, fall to: if you can mock a leek you can eat a leek.

Gow. Enough, captain: you have astonished him.

Flu. I say, I will make him eat some part of my leek, or I will peat his pate four days. Bite, I pray you; it is good for your green wound and your ploody coxcomb.

Pist. Must I bite?

Flu. Yes, certainly, and out of doubt and out of question too and ambiguities.

Pist. By this leek, I will most horribly revenge. I eat and eat, I swear—

Flu. Eat, I pray you. Will you have some more sauce to your leek? there is not enough leek to swear by.

Pist. Quiet thy cudgel; thou dost see I eat.

Flu. Much good do you, scauld knave, heartily. Nay, pray you, throw none away; the skin is good for your broken coxcomb. When you take occasions to see leeks hereafter, I pray you, mock at 'em; that is all.

Pist.   Good.

Flu.   Ay, leeks is good. Hold you, there is a groat to heal your pate.

Pist.   Me a groat!

Flu.   Yes, verily and in truth, you shall take it; or I have another leek in my pocket, which you shall eat.

Pist.   I take thy groat in earnest of revenge.

Flu.   If I owe you any thing I will pay you in cudgels: you shall be a woodmonger, and buy nothing of me but cudgels. God b' wi' you, and keep you, and heal your pate.   [*Exit.*

Pist.   All hell shall stir for this.

Gow.   Go, go; you are a counterfeit cowardly knave. Will you mock at an ancient tradition, begun upon an honourable respect, and worn as a memorable trophy of predeceased valour, and dare not avouch in your deeds any of your words? I have seen you gleeking and galling at this gentleman twice or thrice. You thought, because he could not speak English in the native garb, he could not therefore handle an English cudgel: you find it otherwise; and henceforth let a Welsh correction teach you a good English condition. Fare ye well.

           [*Exit.*

Pist.   Doth Fortune play the huswife with me now?
News have I that my Nell is dead i' the spital
Of malady of France;
And there my rendezvous is quite cut off.
Old I do wax, and from my weary limbs
Honour is cudgelled. Well, bawd I'll turn,
And something lean to cut-purse of quick hand.
To England will I steal, and there I'll steal:

And patches will I get unto these cudgell'd scars,
And swear I got them in the Gallia wars.   [*Exit.*

SCENE II.—*Troyes in Champagne. An Apartment
in the French King's Palace.*

Enter, at one door, KING HENRY, EXETER, BEDFORD,
GLOUCESTER, WARWICK, WESTMORELAND, *and other
Lords; at another, the French King,* QUEEN ISABEL, *the*
PRINCESS KATHARINE, ALICE, *and other Ladies, the* DUKE
of BURGUNDY, *and his Train.*

K. Hen.   Peace to this meeting, wherefore we are met!
Unto our brother France, and to our sister,
Health and fair time of day; joy and good wishes
To our most fair and princely cousin Katharine;
And, as a branch and member of this royalty,
By whom this great assembly is contriv'd,
We do salute you, Duke of Burgundy;
And, princes French, and peers, health to you all!
Fr. King.   Right joyous are we to behold your face,
Most worthy brother England; fairly met:
So are you, princes English, every one.
Q. Isa.   So happy be the issue, brother England,
Of this good day and of this gracious meeting,
As we are now glad to behold your eyes;
Your eyes, which hitherto have borne in them
Against the French, that met them in their bent,
The fatal balls of murdering basilisks:
The venom of such looks, we fairly hope,
Have lost their quality, and that this day
Shall change all griefs and quarrels into love.

K. Hen.　To cry amen to that, thus we appear.

Q. Isa.　You English princes all, I do salute you.

Bur.　My duty to you both, on equal love,
　　Great Kings of France and England! That I have
　　　　labour'd
　　With all my wits, my pains, and strong
　　　　endeavours,
　　To bring your most imperial majesties
　　Unto this bar and royal interview,
　　Your mightiness on both parts best can witness.
　　Since then my office hath so far prevail'd
　　That face to face, and royal eye to eye,
　　You have congreeted, let it not disgrace me
　　If I demand before this royal view,
　　What rub or what impediment there is,
　　Why that the naked, poor, and mangled Peace,
　　Dear nurse of arts, plenties, and joyful births,
　　Should not in this best garden of the world,
　　Our fertile France, put up her lovely visage?
　　Alas! she hath from France too long been chas'd,
　　And all her husbandry doth lie on heaps,
　　Corrupting in it own fertility.
　　Her vine, the merry cheerer of the heart,
　　Unpruned dies; her hedges even-pleach'd,
　　Like prisoners wildly overgrown with hair,
　　Put forth disorder'd twigs; her fallow leas
　　The darnel, hemlock and rank fumitory
　　Doth root upon, while that the coulter rusts
　　That should deracinate such savagery;
　　The even mead, that erst brought sweetly forth
　　The freckled cowslip, burnet, and green clover,

Wanting the scythe, all uncorrected, rank,
Conceives by idleness, and nothing teems
But hateful docks, rough thistles, kecksies, burrs,
Losing both beauty and utility.
And as our vineyards, fallows, meads, and hedges,
Defective in their natures, grow to wildness,
Even so our houses and ourselves and children
Have lost, or do not learn for want of time,
The sciences that should become our country,
But grow like savages, as soldiers will
That nothing do but meditate on blood,
To swearing and stern looks, defus'd attire,
And every thing that seems unnatural.
Which to reduce into our former favour
You are assembled; and my speech entreats
That I may know the let, why gentle Peace
Should not expel these inconveniences,
And bless us with her former qualities.

K. Hen.   If, Duke of Burgundy, you would the peace,
Whose want gives growth to the imperfections
Which you have cited, you must buy that peace
With full accord to all our just demands;
Whose tenours and particular effects
You have, enschedul'd briefly, in your hands.

Bur.   The king hath heard them; to the which as yet
There is no answer made.

K. Hen.   Well then the peace,
Which you before so urg'd, lies in his answer.

Fr. King.   I have but with a cursorary eye
O'erglanc'd the articles: pleaseth your grace
To appoint some of your council presently

To sit with us once more, with better heed
To re-survey them, we will suddenly
Pass our accept and peremptory answer.

K. Hen.   Brother, we shall. Go, uncle Exeter,
And brother Clarence, and you, brother Gloucester,
Warwick and Huntingdon, go with the king;
And take with you free power to ratify,
Augment, or alter, as your wisdoms best
Shall see advantageable for our dignity,
Any thing in or out of our demands,
And we 'll consign thereto. Will you, fair sister,
Go with the princes, or stay here with us?

Q. Isa.   Our gracious brother, I will go with them.
Haply a woman's voice may do some good
When articles too nicely urg'd be stood on.

K. Hen.   Yet leave our cousin Katharine here with us:
She is our capital demand, compris'd
Within the fore-rank of our articles.

Q. Isa.   She hath good leave.

> [*Exeunt all but King Henry, Katharine, and Alice.*

K. Hen.   Fair Katharine, and most fair,
Will you vouchsafe to teach a soldier terms
Such as will enter at a lady's ear
And plead his love-suit to her gentle heart?

Kath.   Your majesty shall mock at me; I cannot speak your
England.

K. Hen.   O fair Katharine! if you will love me soundly
with your French heart, I will be glad to hear you confess it brokenly with your English tongue. Do you like
me, Kate?

Kath.   *Pardonnez-moy,* I cannot tell vat is "like me."

K. Hen.   An angel is like you, Kate, and you are like an angel.

Kath.   *Que dit-il? que je suis semblable à les anges?*

Alice.   *Ouy, vrayment, sauf vostre grace, ainsi dit-il.*

K. Hen.   I said so, dear Katharine, and I must not blush to affirm it.

Kath.   *O bon Dieu! les langues des hommes sont pleines de trom-peries.*

K. Hen.   What says she, fair one? that the tongues of men are full of deceits?

Alice.   *Ouy;* dat de tongues of de mans is be full of deceits: dat is de princess.

K. Hen.   The princess is the better Englishwoman. I' faith, Kate, my wooing is fit for thy understanding: I am glad thou canst speak no better English; for if thou could'st, thou would'st find me such a plain king that thou would'st think I had sold my farm to buy my crown. I know no ways to mince it in love, but directly to say "I love you": then if you urge me farther than to say "Do you in faith?" I wear out my suit. Give me your answer; i' faith, do: and so clap hands and a bargain. How say you, lady?

Kath.   *Sauf vostre honneur,* me understand vell.

K. Hen.   Marry, if you would put me to verses, or to dance for your sake, Kate, why you undid me: for the one, I have neither words nor measure, and for the other, I have no strength in measure, yet a reasonable measure in strength. If I could win a lady at leap-frog, or by vaulting into my saddle with my armour on my back, under the correction of bragging be it spoken, I should quickly leap into a wife. Or if I might buffet for my love, or

bound my horse for her favours, I could lay on like a
butcher and sit like a jack-an-apes, never off. But, before
God, Kate, I cannot look greenly nor gasp out my eloquence, nor I have no cunning in protestation; only
downright oaths, which I never use till urged, nor never
break for urging. If thou canst love a fellow of this temper, Kate, whose face is not worth sun-burning, that
never looks in his glass for love of any thing he sees
there, let thine eye be thy cook. I speak to thee plain
soldier: if thou canst love me for this, take me; if not,
to say to thee that I shall die, is true; but for thy love, by
the Lord, no; yet I love thee too. And while thou livest,
dear Kate, take a fellow of plain and uncoined constancy,
for he perforce must do thee right, because he hath not
the gift to woo in other places; for these fellows of infinite tongue, that can rime themselves into ladies' favours, they do always reason themselves out again.
What! a speaker is but a prater; a rime is but a ballad.
A good leg will fall, a straight back will stoop, a black
beard will turn white, a curled pate will grow bald, a fair
face will wither, a full eye will wax hollow; but a good
heart, Kate, is the sun and the moon; or rather the sun,
and not the moon; for it shines bright and never changes,
but keeps his course truly. If thou would have such a
one, take me; and take me, take a soldier; take a soldier,
take a king. And what sayest thou then to my love?
speak, my fair, and fairly, I pray thee.

Kath. Is it possible dat I sould love de enemy of France?

K. Hen. No; it is not possible you should love the enemy
of France, Kate; but, in loving me, you should love the
friend of France, for I love France so well that I will not

"Is it possible dat I sould love de enemy of France?"

part with a village of it; I will have it all mine: and Kate, when France is mine and I am yours, then yours is France and you are mine.

Kath. I cannot tell vat is dat.

K. Hen. No, Kate? I will tell thee in French, which I am sure will hang upon my tongue like a new-married wife about her husband's neck, hardly to be shook off. *Je quand sur le possession de France, et quand vous avez le possession de moy*—let me see, what then? Saint Denis be my speed!—*donc vostre est France, et vous estes mienne.* It is as easy for me, Kate, to conquer the kingdom as to speak so much more French: I shall never move thee in French, unless it be to laugh at me.

Kath. *Sauf vostre honneur, le François que vous parlez il est meilleur que l'Anglois lequel je parle.*

K. Hen. No, faith, is't not, Kate; but thy speaking of my tongue, and I thine, most truly-falsely, must needs be granted to be much at one. But, Kate, dost thou understand thus much English? Canst thou love me?

Kath. I cannot tell.

K. Hen. Can any of your neighbours tell, Kate? I'll ask them. Come, I know thou lovest me: and at night when you come into your closet you'll question this gentlewoman about me; and I know, Kate, you will to her dispraise those parts in me that you love with your heart: but, good Kate, mock me mercifully; the rather, gentle princess, because I love thee cruelly. If ever thou be'st mine, Kate, as I have a saving faith within me tells me thou shalt, I get thee with scambling, and thou must therefore needs prove a good soldier-breeder. Shall not thou and I, between Saint Denis and Saint George, compound a boy, half French, half English, that shall go to Constantinople and take the Turk by the beard? shall we not? what sayest thou, my fair flower-de-luce?

Kath.　I do not know dat.

K. Hen.　No; 'tis hereafter to know, but now to promise: do but now promise, Kate, you will endeavour for your French part of such a boy, and for my English moiety take the word of a king and a bachelor. How answer you, *la plus belle Katharine du monde, mon tres cher et divin déesse?*

Kath.　Your *majesté* ave *fausse* French enough to deceive de most *sage* damoiselle dat is *en* France.

K. Hen.　Now, fie upon my false French! By mine honour, in true English, I love thee, Kate: by which honour I dare not swear thou lovest me; yet my blood begins to flatter me that thou dost, notwithstanding the poor and untempering effect of my visage. Now beshrew my father's ambition! he was thinking of civil wars when he got me: therefore was I created with a stubborn outside, with an aspect of iron, that when I come to woo ladies I fright them. But, in faith, Kate, the elder I wax the better I shall appear: my comfort is, that old age, that ill layer-up of beauty, can do no more spoil upon my face: thou hast me, if thou hast me, at the worst; and thou shalt wear me, if thou wear me, better and better. And therefore tell me, most fair Katharine, will you have me? Put off your maiden blushes; avouch the thoughts of your heart with the looks of an empress; take me by the hand, and say "Harry of England, I am thine": which word thou shalt no sooner bless mine ear withal, but I will tell thee aloud "England is thine, Ireland is thine, France is thine, and Henry Plantagenet is thine"; who, though I speak it before his face, if he be not fellow with the best king, thou shalt find the best king of good fellows. Come, your answer in broken music; for thy voice is music, and thy English broken; therefore, queen of all, Katharine, break thy mind to me in broken English: wilt thou have me?

Kath.　Dat is as it sall please de *roy mon père.*

K. Hen.　Nay, it will please him well, Kate; it shall please him, Kate.

Kath.　Den it sall also content me.

K. Hen.　Upon that I kiss your hand, and I call you my queen.

Kath.　*Laissez, mon seigneur, laissez, laissez! Ma foy, je ne veux point que vous abaissiez vostre grandeur, en baisant la main d'une de vostre seigneurie indigne serviteur: excusez moy, je vous supplie, mon très puissant seigneur.*

K. Hen.　Then I will kiss your lips, Kate.

Kath.　*Les dames et damoiselles, pour estre baisées devant leur nopces, il n'est pas le coutume de France.*

K. Hen.　Madam my interpreter, what says she?

Alice.　Dat it is not be de fashion *pour* les ladies of France —I cannot tell vat is *baiser* in English.

K. Hen.　To kiss.

Alice.　Your majesty *entendre bettre que moy.*

K. Hen.　It is not a fashion for the maids in France to kiss before they are married, would she say?

Alice.　*Ouy, vraiment.*

K. Hen.　O Kate! nice customs curtsy to great kings. Dear Kate, you and I cannot be confined within the weak list of a country's fashion: we are the makers of manners, Kate; and the liberty that follows our places stops the mouth of all find-faults, as I will do yours, for upholding the nice fashion of your country in denying me a kiss: therefore, patiently and yielding. [*Kissing her.*] You have witchcraft in your lips, Kate: there is more eloquence in a sugar touch of them than in the tongues of the French council; and they should sooner persuade Harry of England than a general petition of monarchs. Here comes your father.

Re-enter the French King and his Queen, BURGUNDY, *and other Lords.*

Bur. God save your majesty! My royal cousin, teach you our princess English?

K. Hen. I would have her learn, my fair cousin, how perfectly I love her; and that is good English.

Bur. Is she not apt?

K. Hen. Our tongue is rough, coz, and my condition is not smooth; so that, having neither the voice nor the heart of flattery about me, I cannot so conjure up the spirit of love in her, that he will appear in his true likeness.

Bur. Pardon the frankness of my mirth if I answer you for that. If you would conjure in her, you must make a circle; if conjure up love in her in his true likeness, he must appear naked and blind. Can you blame her then, being a maid yet rosed over with the virgin crimson of modesty, if she deny the appearance of a naked blind boy in her naked seeing self? It were, my lord, a hard condition for a maid to consign to.

K. Hen. Yet they do wink and yield, as love is blind and enforces.

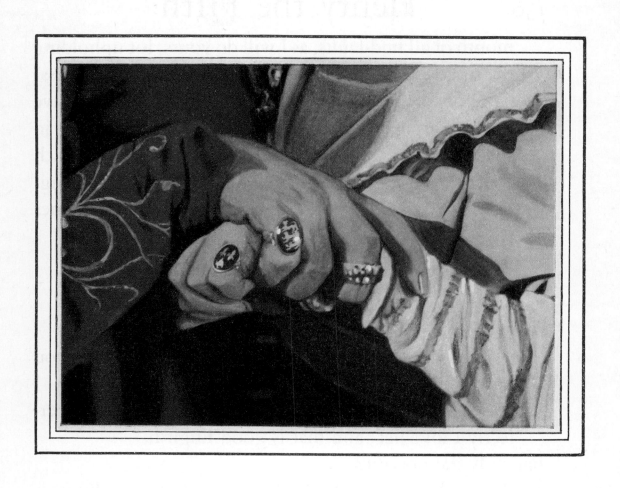

"Shall not thou and I, between Saint Denis and Saint George, compound a boy, half French, half English"

Bur. They are then excused, my lord, when they see not what they do.

K. Hen. Then, good my lord, teach your cousin to consent winking.

Bur. I will wink on her to consent, my lord, if you will teach her to know my meaning: for maids, well summered and warm kept, are like flies at Bartholomew-tide, blind, though they have their eyes; and then they will endure handling, which before would not abide looking on.

K. Hen. This moral ties me over to time and a hot summer; and so I shall catch the fly, your cousin, in the latter end, and she must be blind too.

Bur. As love is, my lord, before it loves.

K. Hen. It is so: and you may, some of you, thank love for my blindness, who cannot see many a fair French city for one fair French maid that stands in my way.

Fr. King. Yes, my lord, you see them perspectively, the cities turned into a maid; for they are all girdled with maiden walls that war hath never entered.

K. Hen. Shall Kate be my wife?

Fr. King. So please you.

K. Hen. I am content; so the maiden cities you talk of may wait on her: so the maid that stood in the way for my wish shall show me the way to my will.

Fr. King We have consented to all terms of reason.

K. Hen. Is 't so, my lords of England?

West. The king hath granted every article:
His daughter first, and then in sequel all,
According to their firm proposed natures.

Exe. Only he hath not yet subscribed this:

Where your majesty demands, that the King of France,
having any occasion to write for matter of grant, shall
name your highness in this form, and with this addition
in French, *Nostre très cher filz Henry, Roy d' Angleterre, Héri-
tier de France*; and thus in Latin, *Præclarissimus filius noster
Henricus, Rex Angliæ, et Hæres Franciæ.*

Fr. King.   Nor this I have not, brother, so denied,
But your request shall make me let it pass.

K. Hen.   I pray you then, in love and dear alliance,
Let that one article rank with the rest;
And thereupon give me your daughter.

Fr. King.   Take her, fair son; and from her blood raise up
Issue to me; that the contending kingdoms
Of France and England, whose very shores look pale
With envy of each other's happiness,
May cease their hatred, and this dear conjunction
Plant neighbourhood and Christian-like accord
In their sweet bosoms, that never war advance
His bleeding sword 'twixt England and fair France.

All.   Amen.

K. Hen.   Now welcome, Kate: and bear me witness all,
That here I kiss her as my sovereign queen.

                                       [*Flourish.*

Q. Isa.   God, the best maker of all marriages,
Combine your hearts in one, your realms in one!
As man and wife, being two, are one in love,
So be there 'twixt your kingdoms such a spousal
That never may ill office, or fell jealousy,
Which troubles oft the bed of blessed marriage,
Thrust in between the paction of these kingdoms,
To make divorce of their incorporate league;

"The cities are all girdled with maiden walls
that war hath never entered"

That English may as French, French Englishmen,
    Receive each other! God speak this Amen!

All.   Amen!

K. Hen.   Prepare we for our marriage: on which day,
    My Lord of Burgundy, we'll take your oath,
    And all the peers', for surety of our leagues.
    Then shall I swear to Kate, and you to me;
    And may our oaths well kept and prosperous be!

                  [Sennet. Exeunt.

Enter CHORUS.

Thus far, with rough and all-unable pen,
    Our bending author hath pursu'd the story;
In little room confining mighty men,
    Mangling by starts the full course of their glory.
Small time, but in that small most greatly liv'd
    This star of England: Fortune made his sword,
By which the world's best garden he achiev'd,
    And of it left his son imperial lord.
Henry the Sixth, in infant bands crown'd King
    Of France and England, did this king succeed;
Whose state so many had the managing,
    That they lost France and made his England bleed:
Which oft our stage hath shown; and, for their sake,
    In your fair minds let this acceptance take.

                  [Exit.